I am grateful to God for everything! I feel complete when I can do something that brings meaning and joy to other lives. I dedicate in these pages much love and affection to others.

Mel Leblanc
2024

This Book Belongs to:

Test Color Page

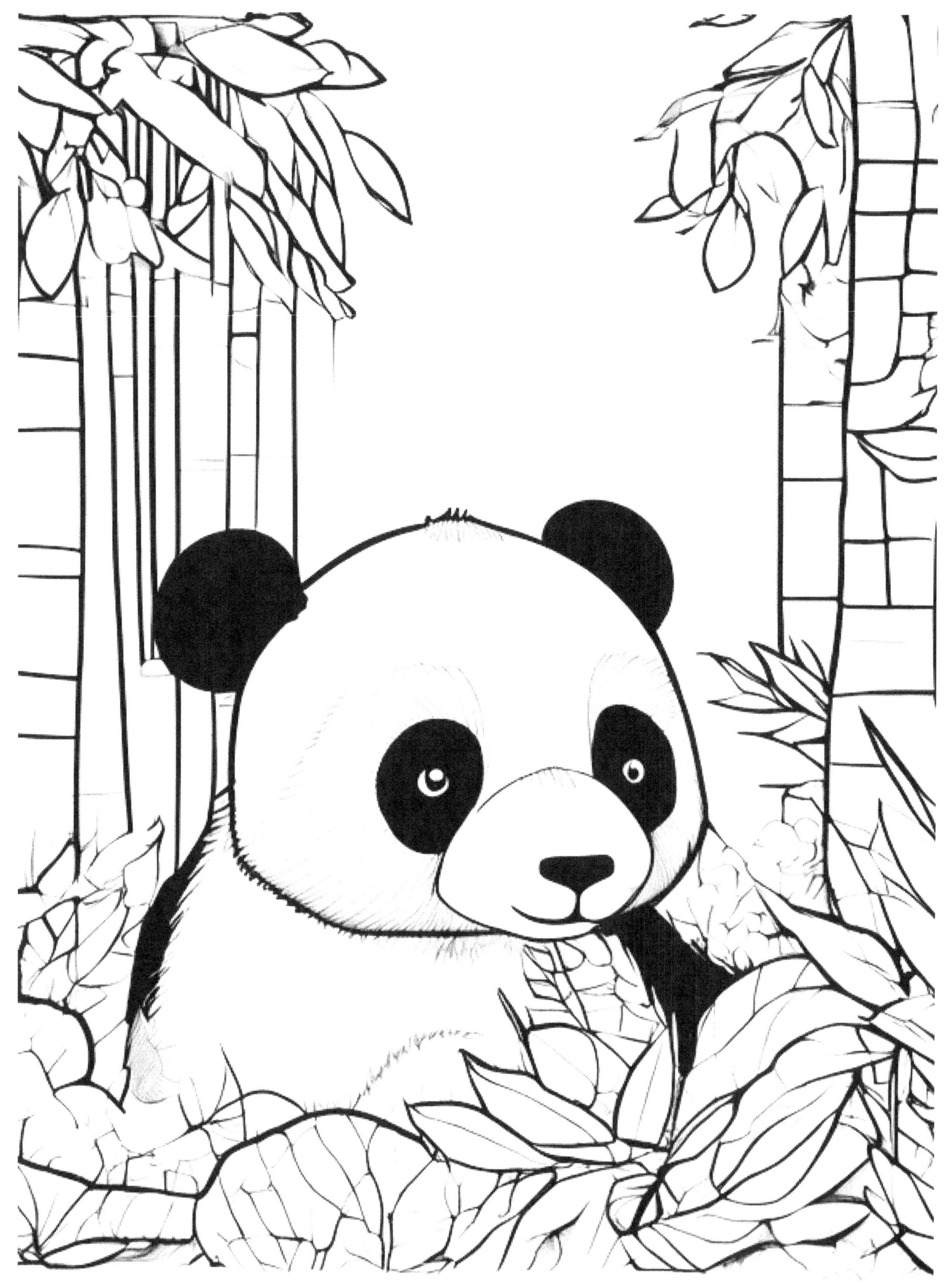

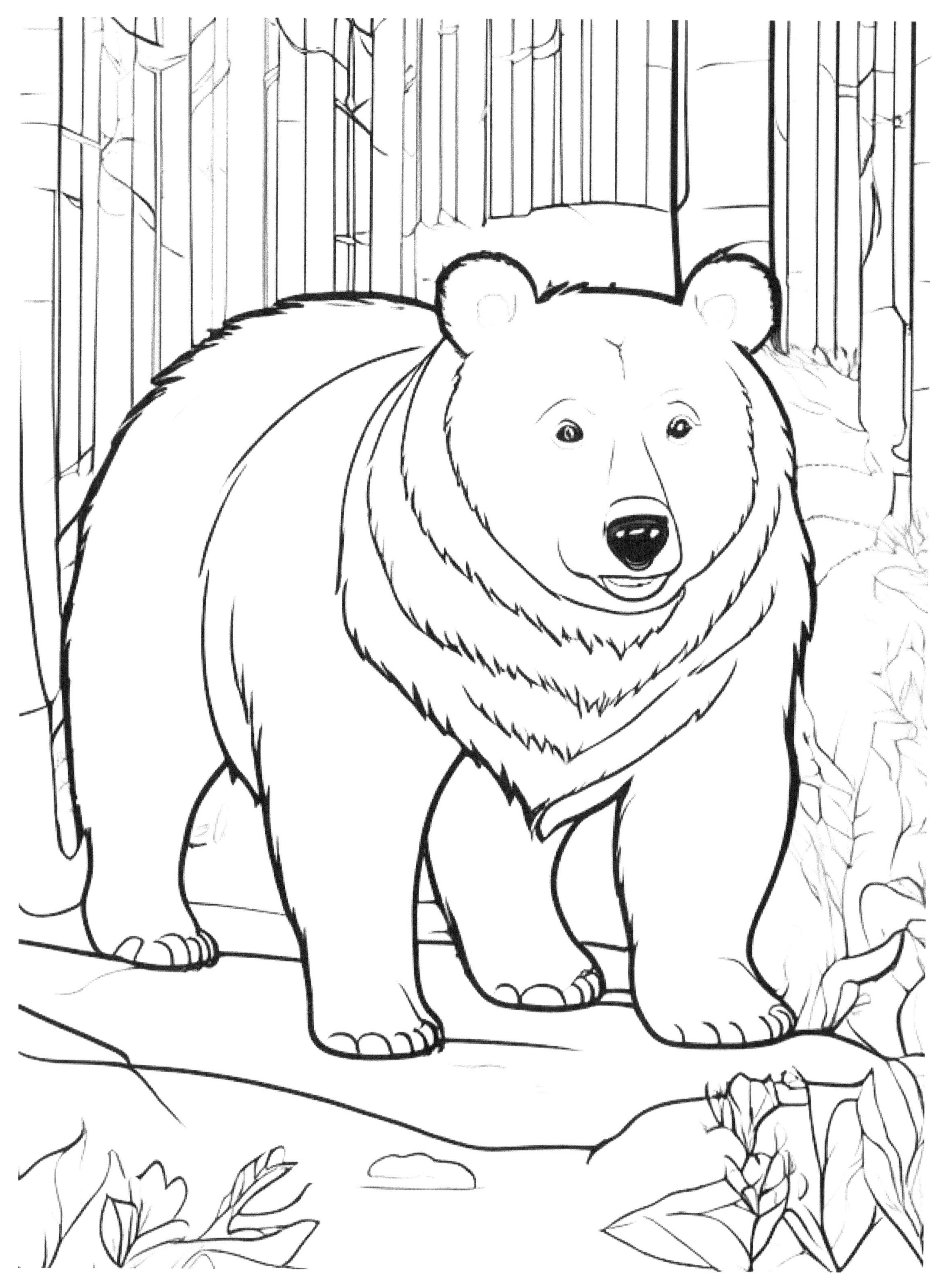

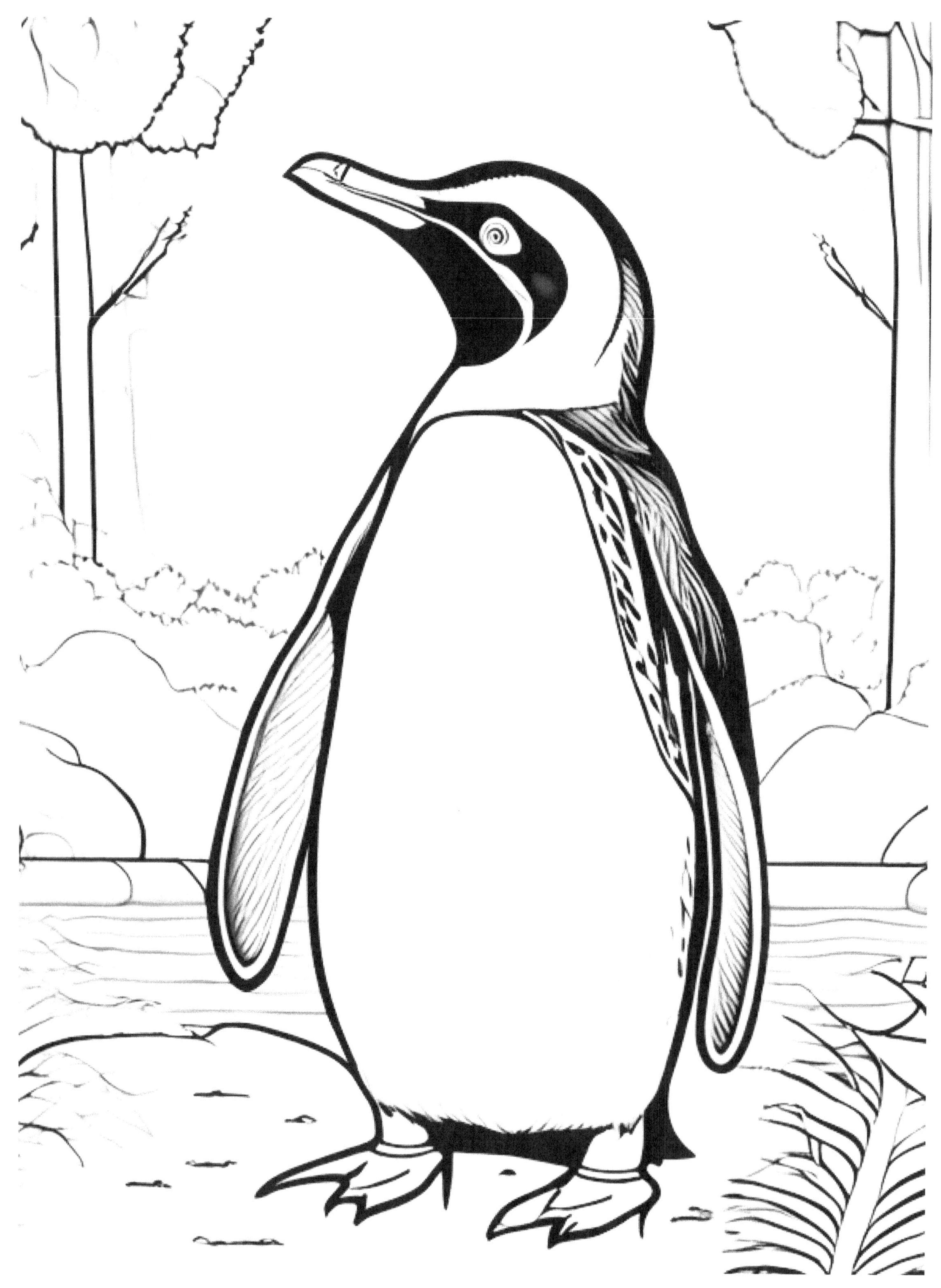

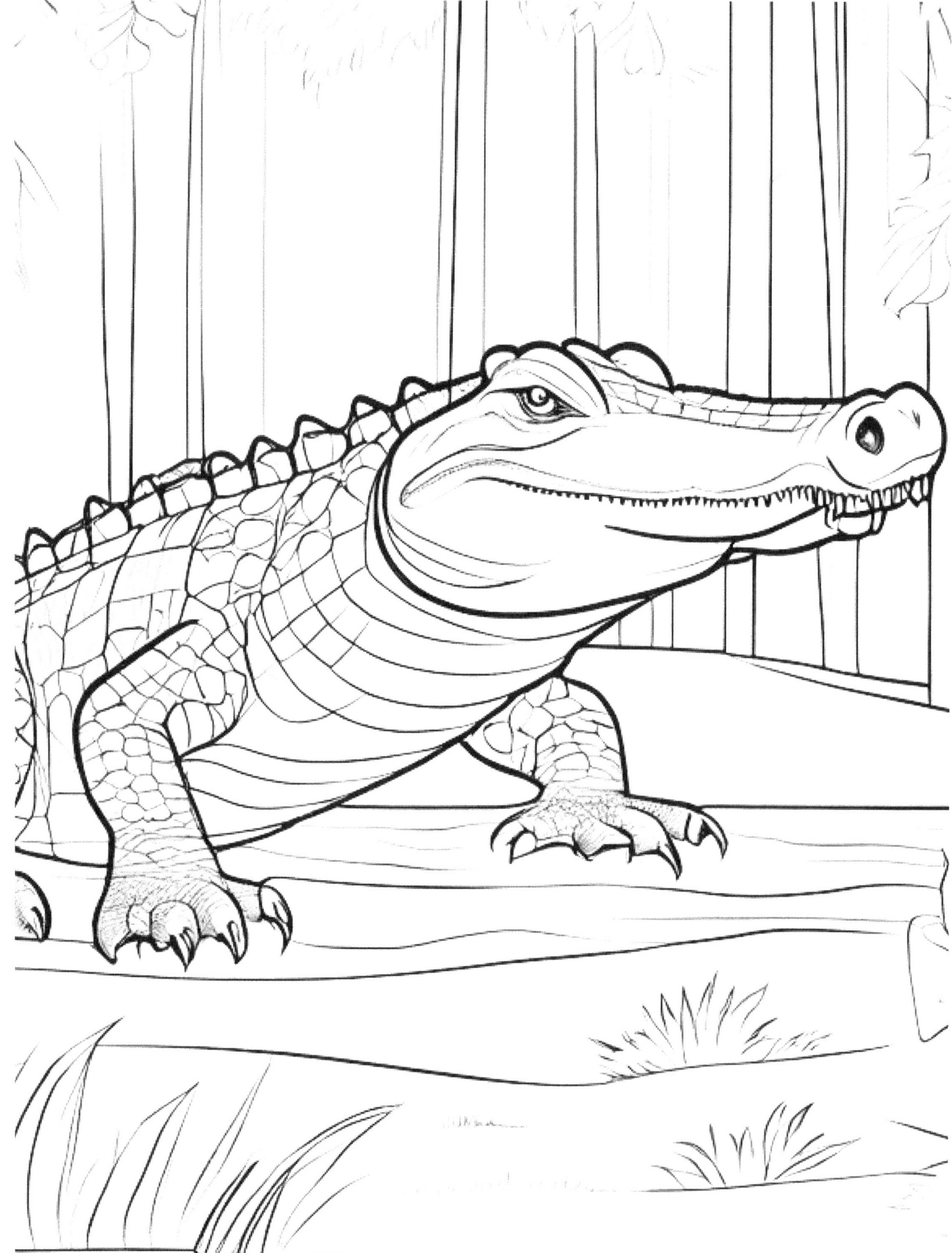

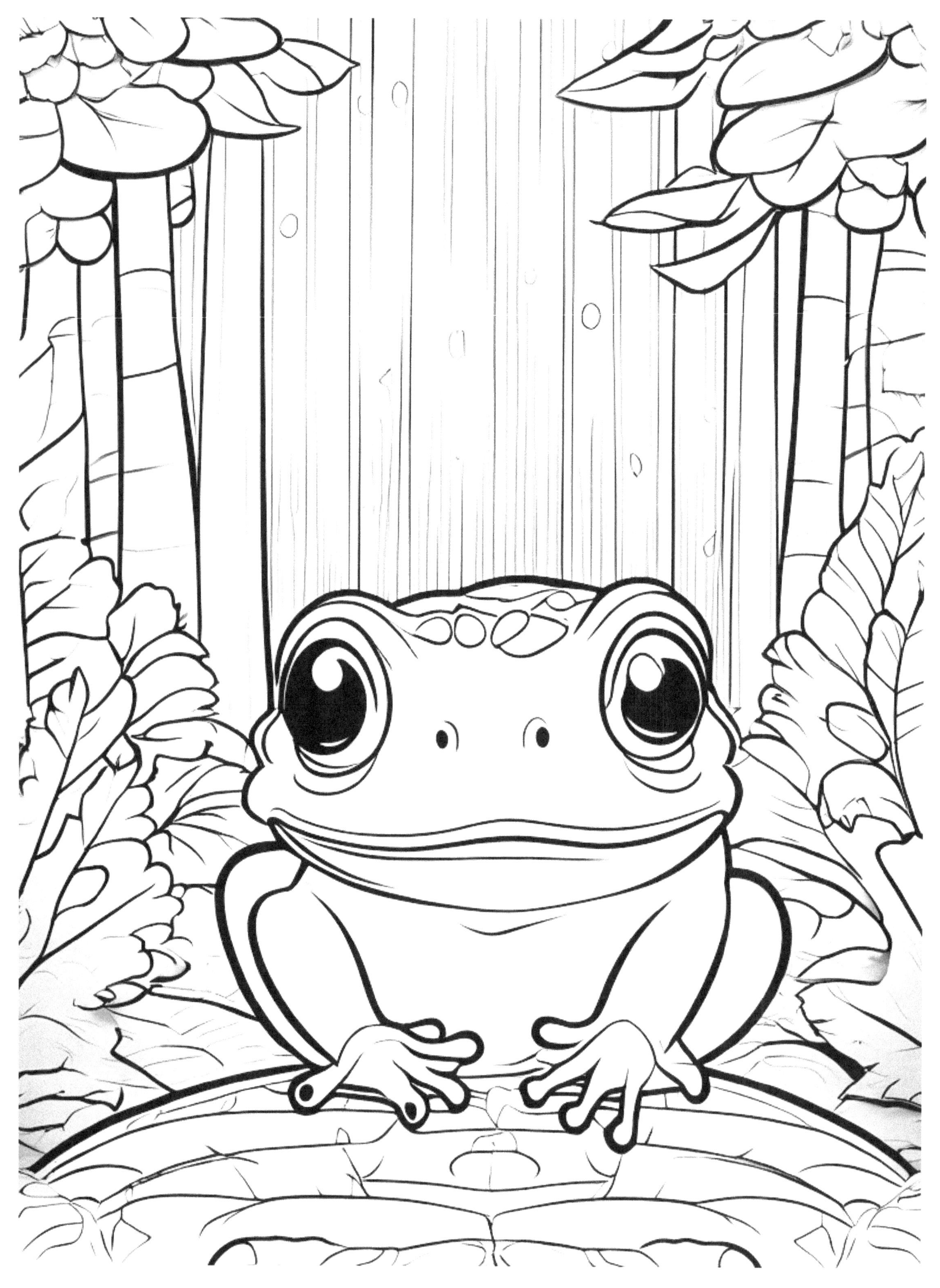

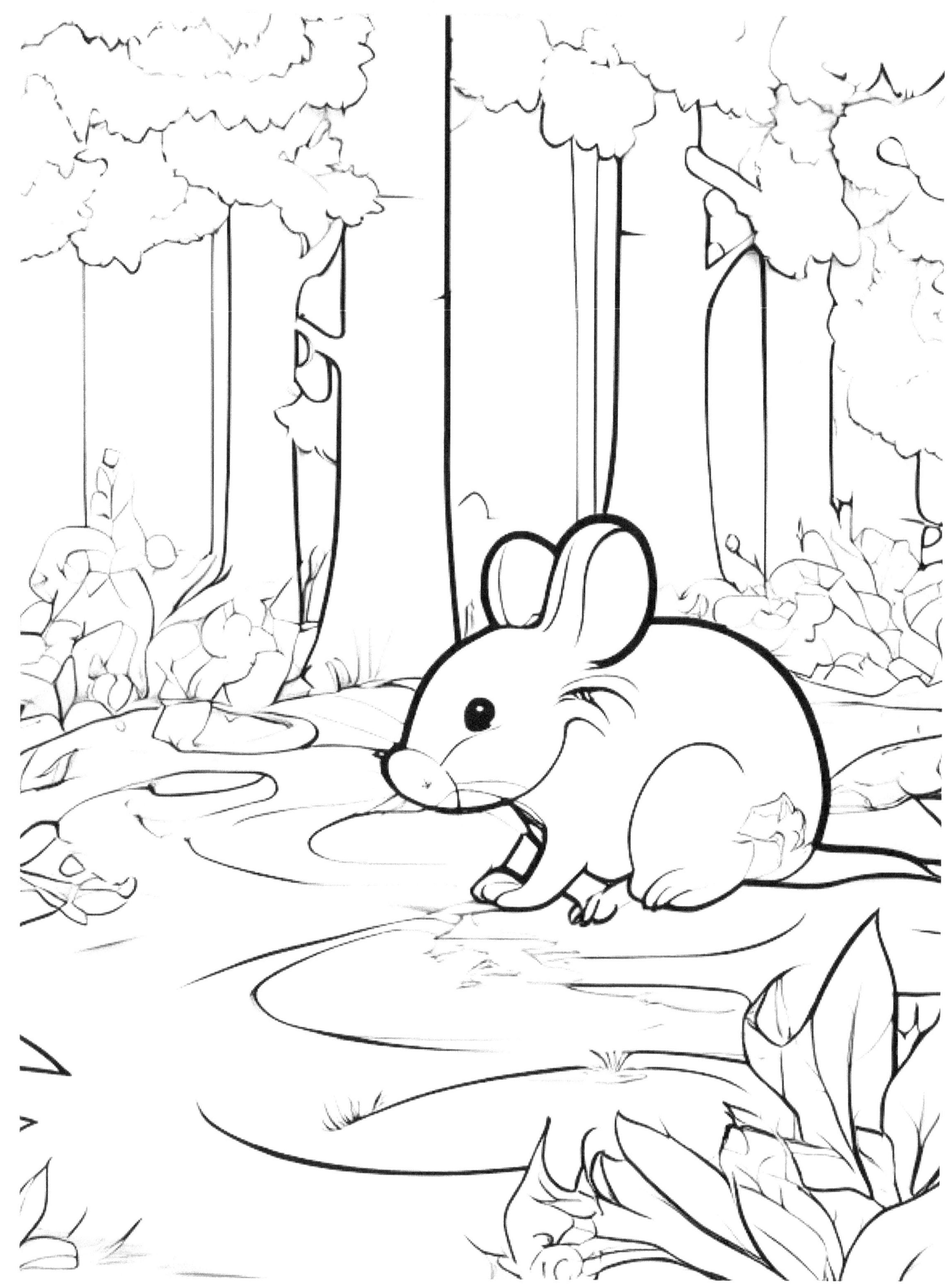

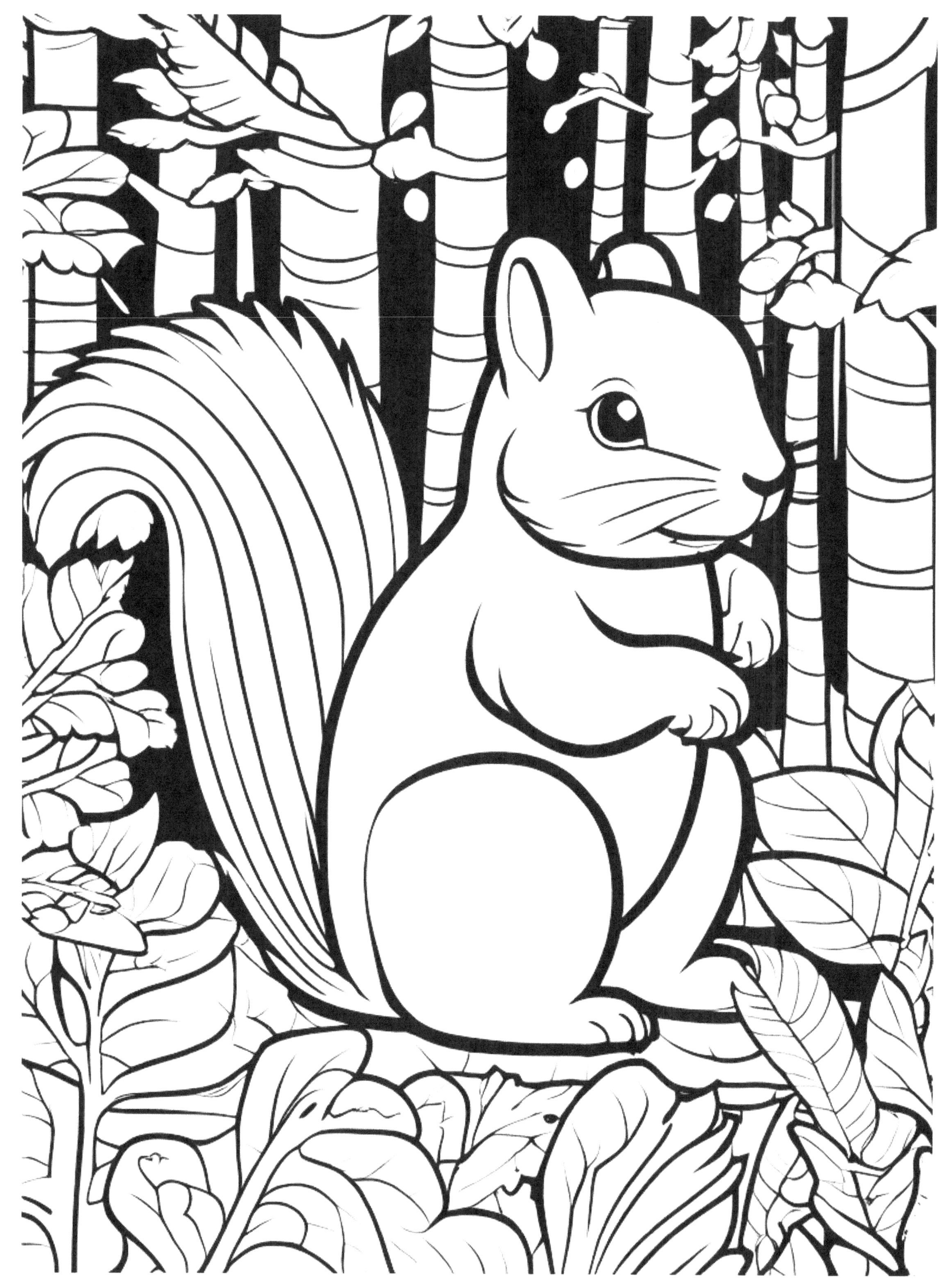

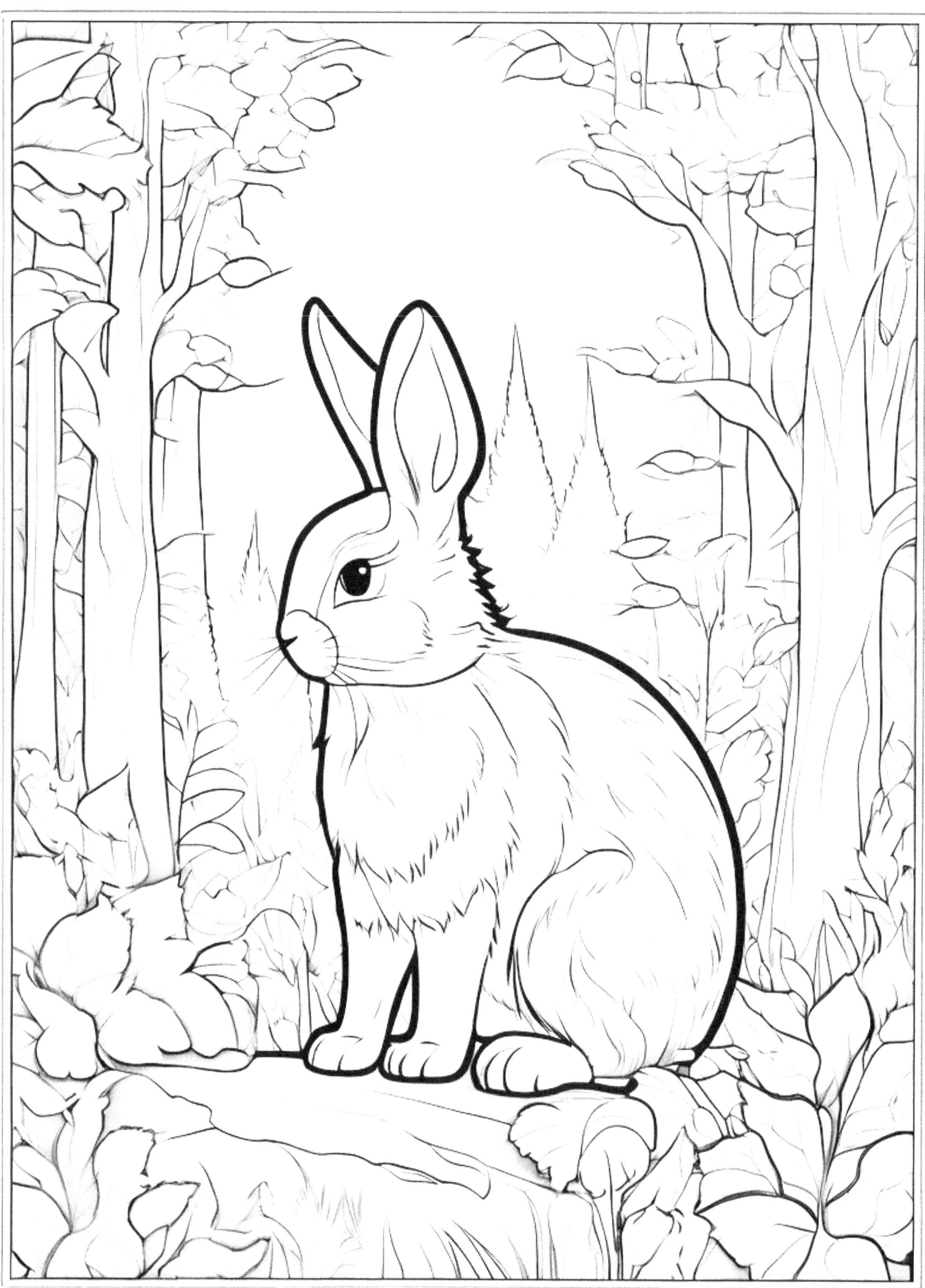

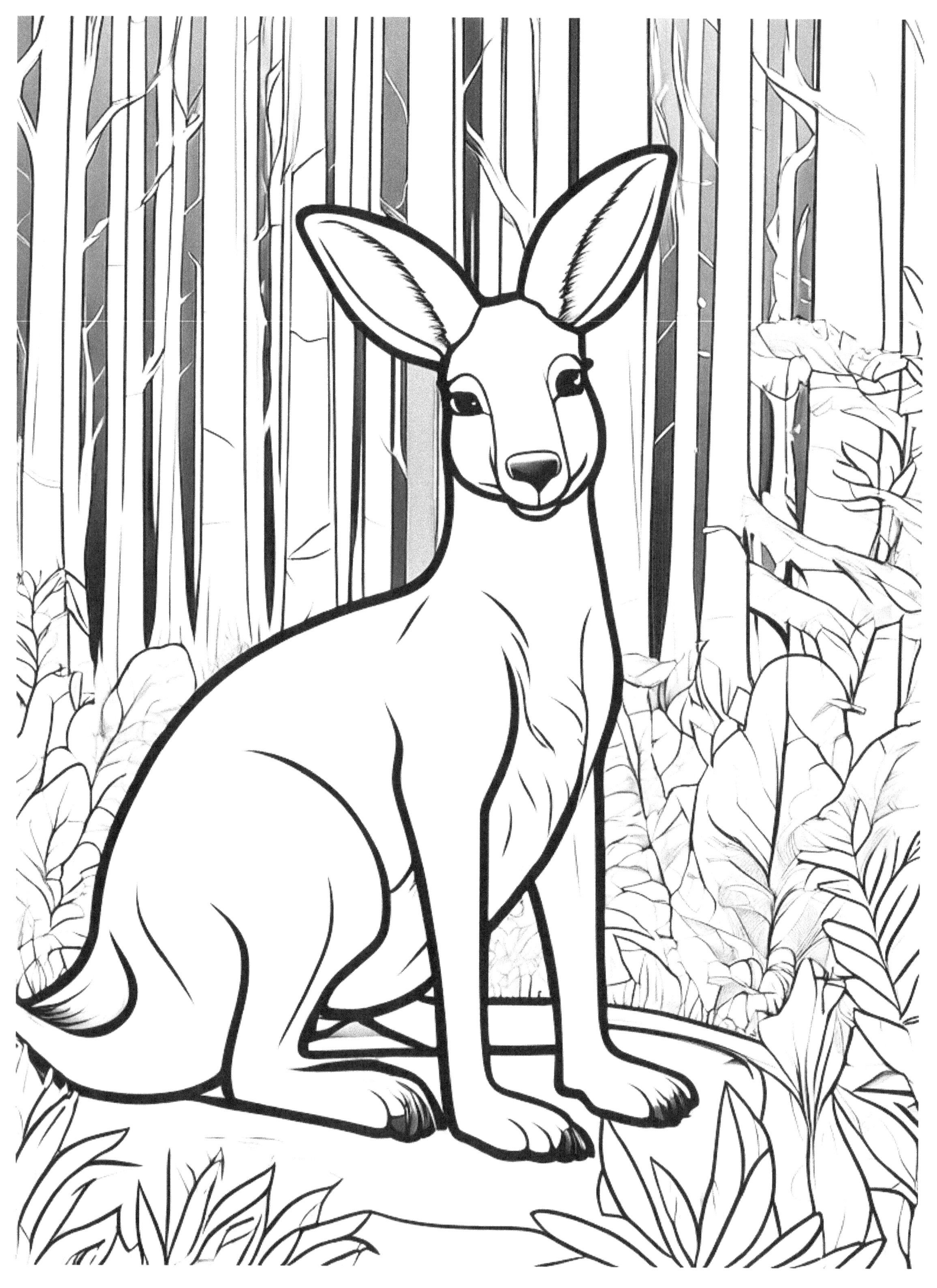

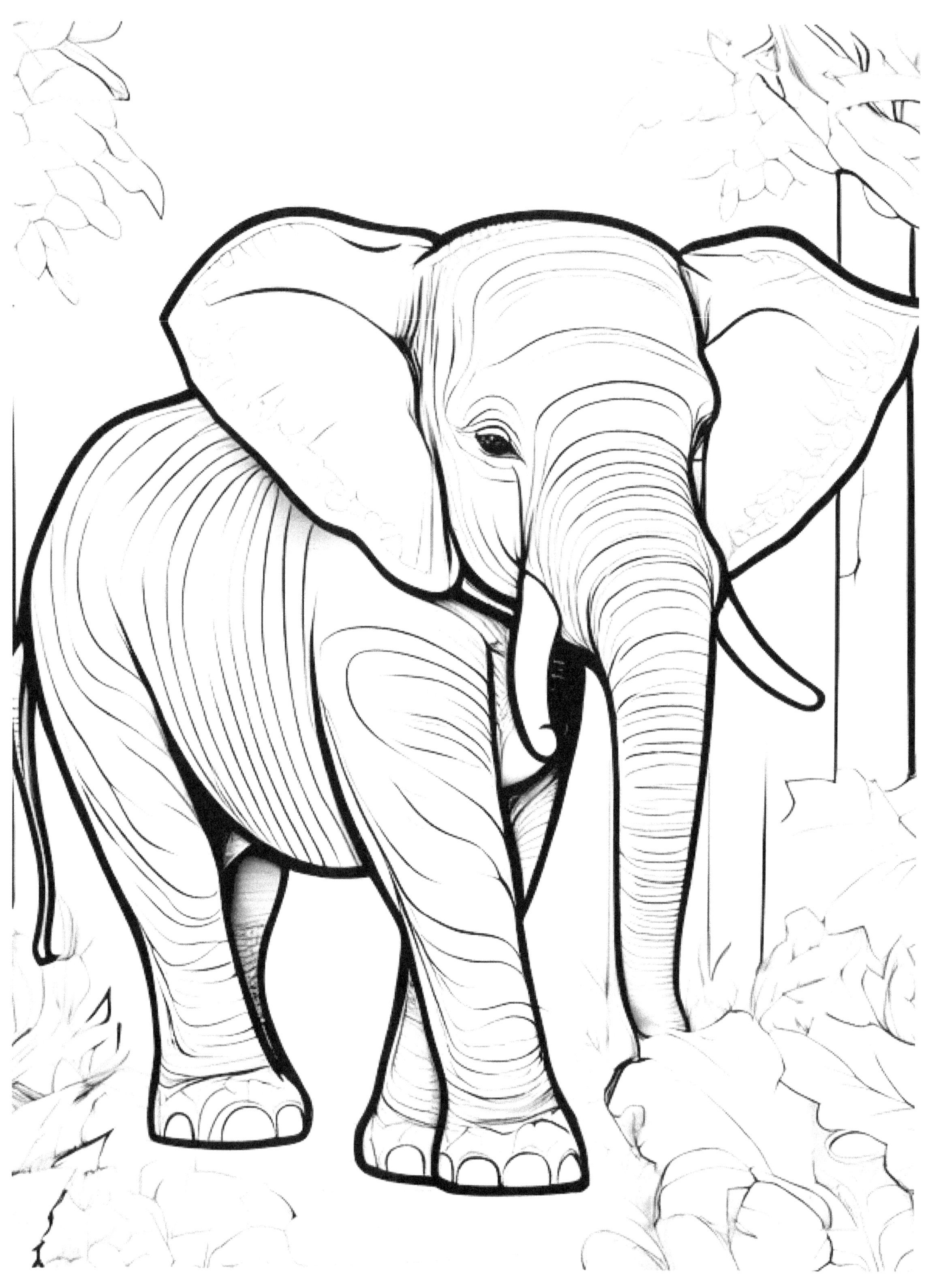

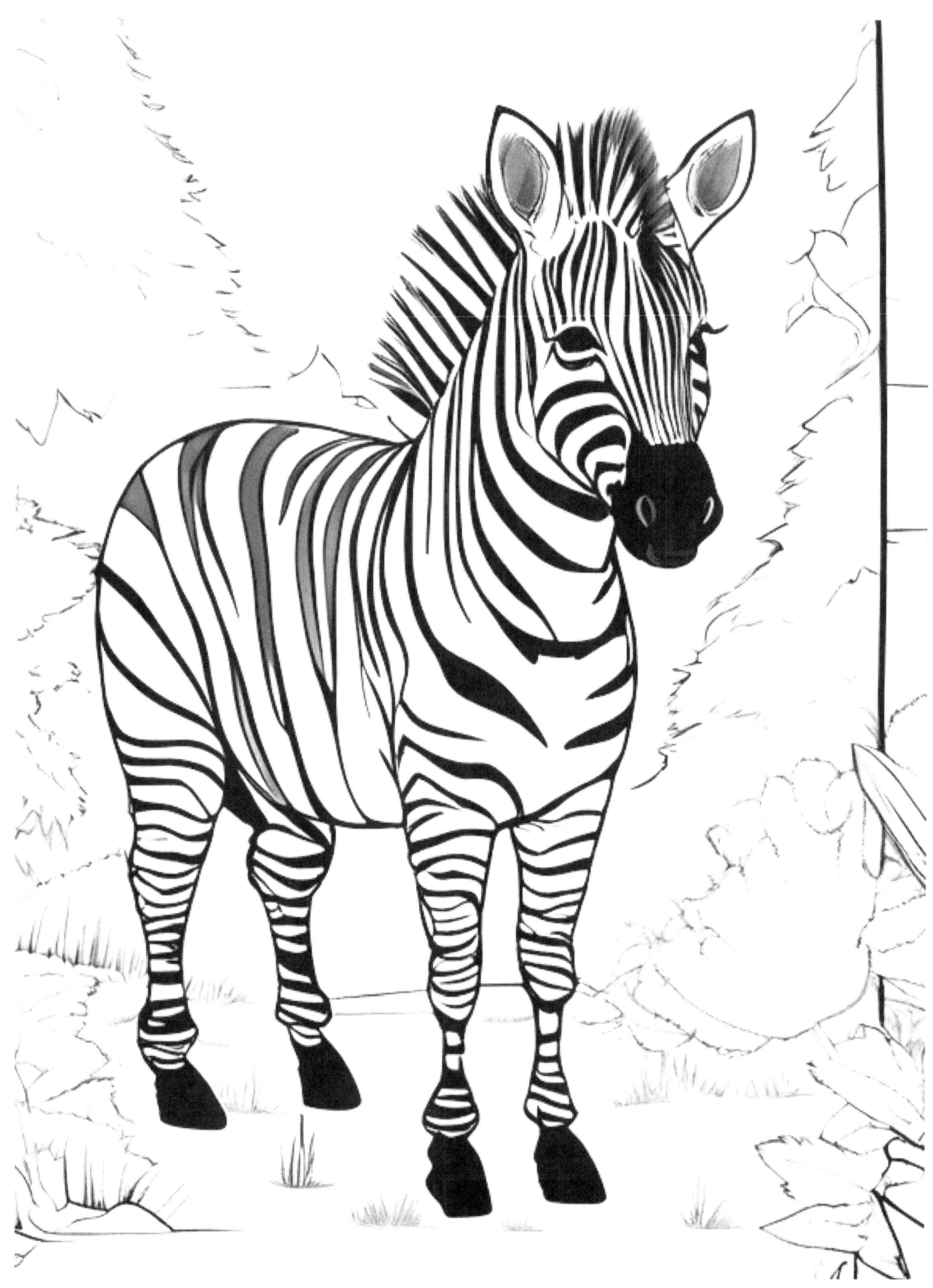

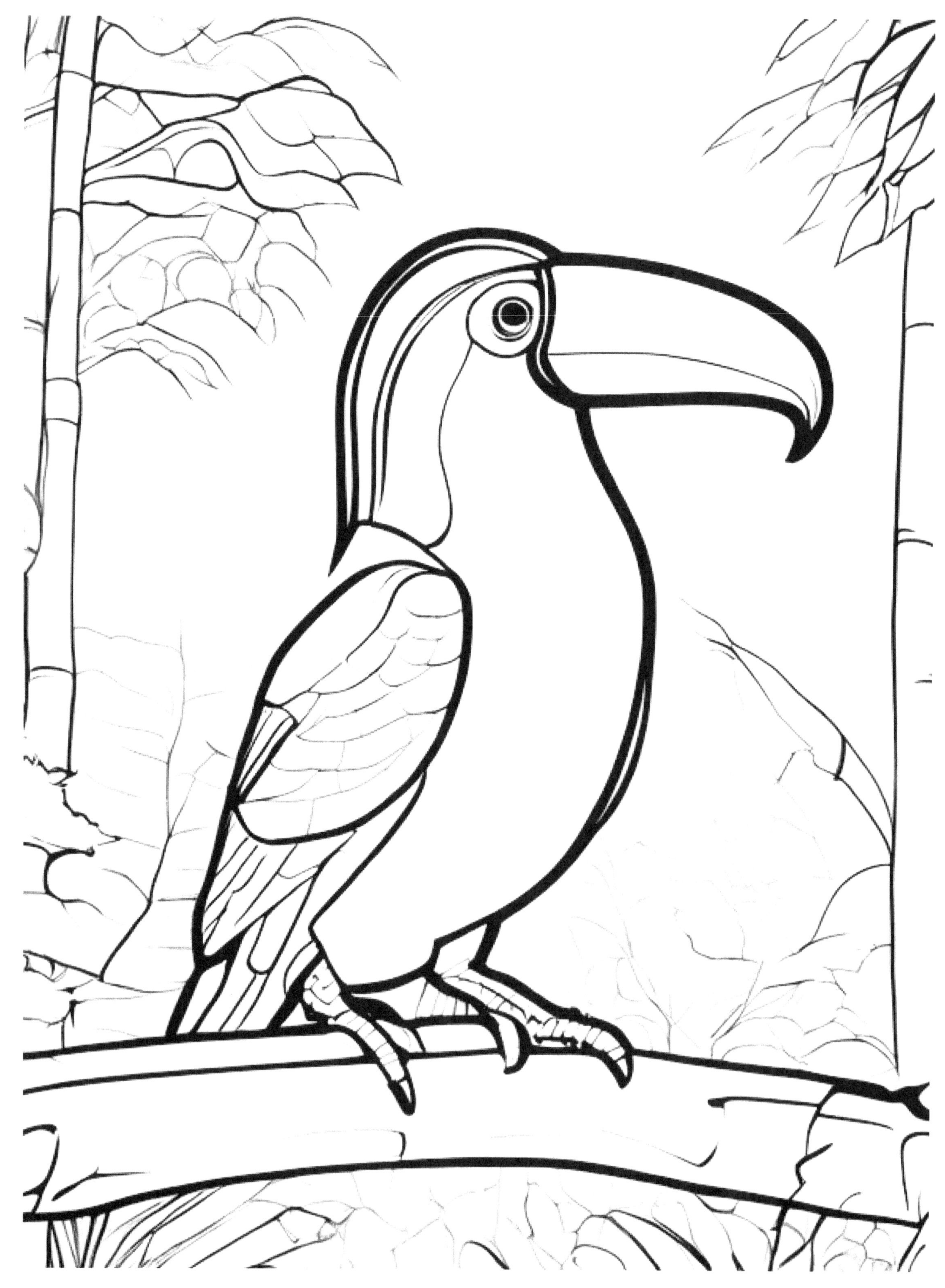

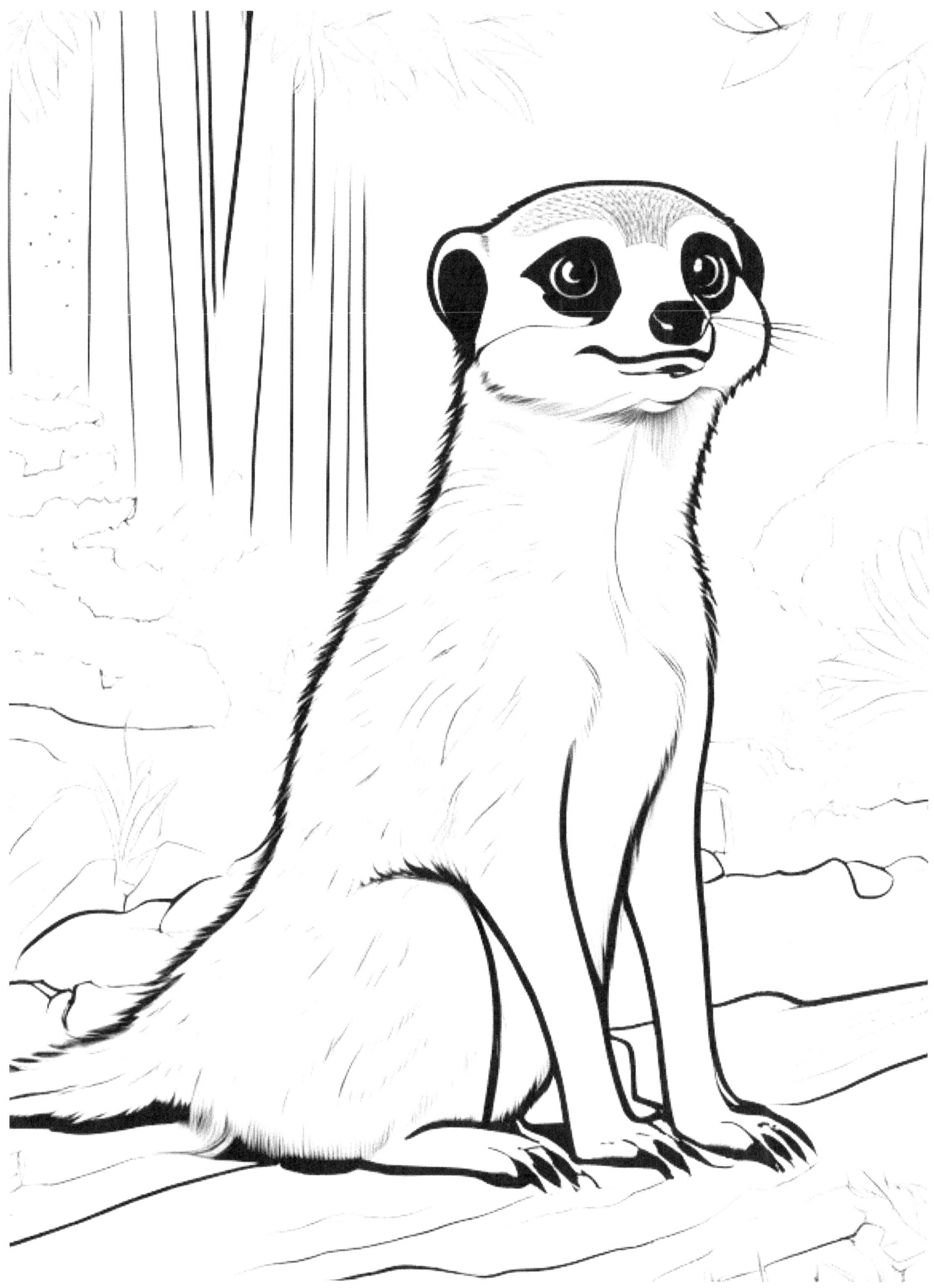

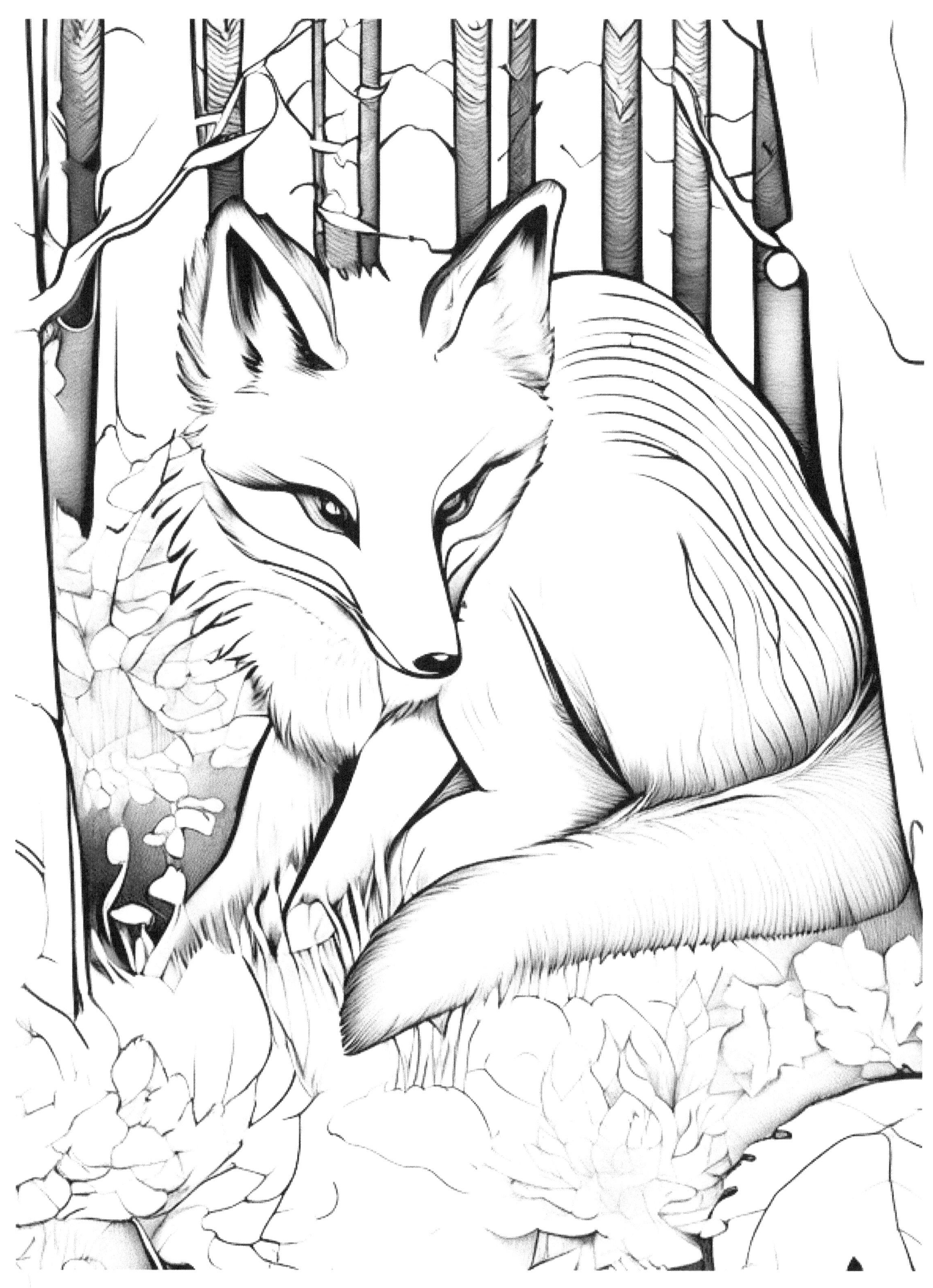

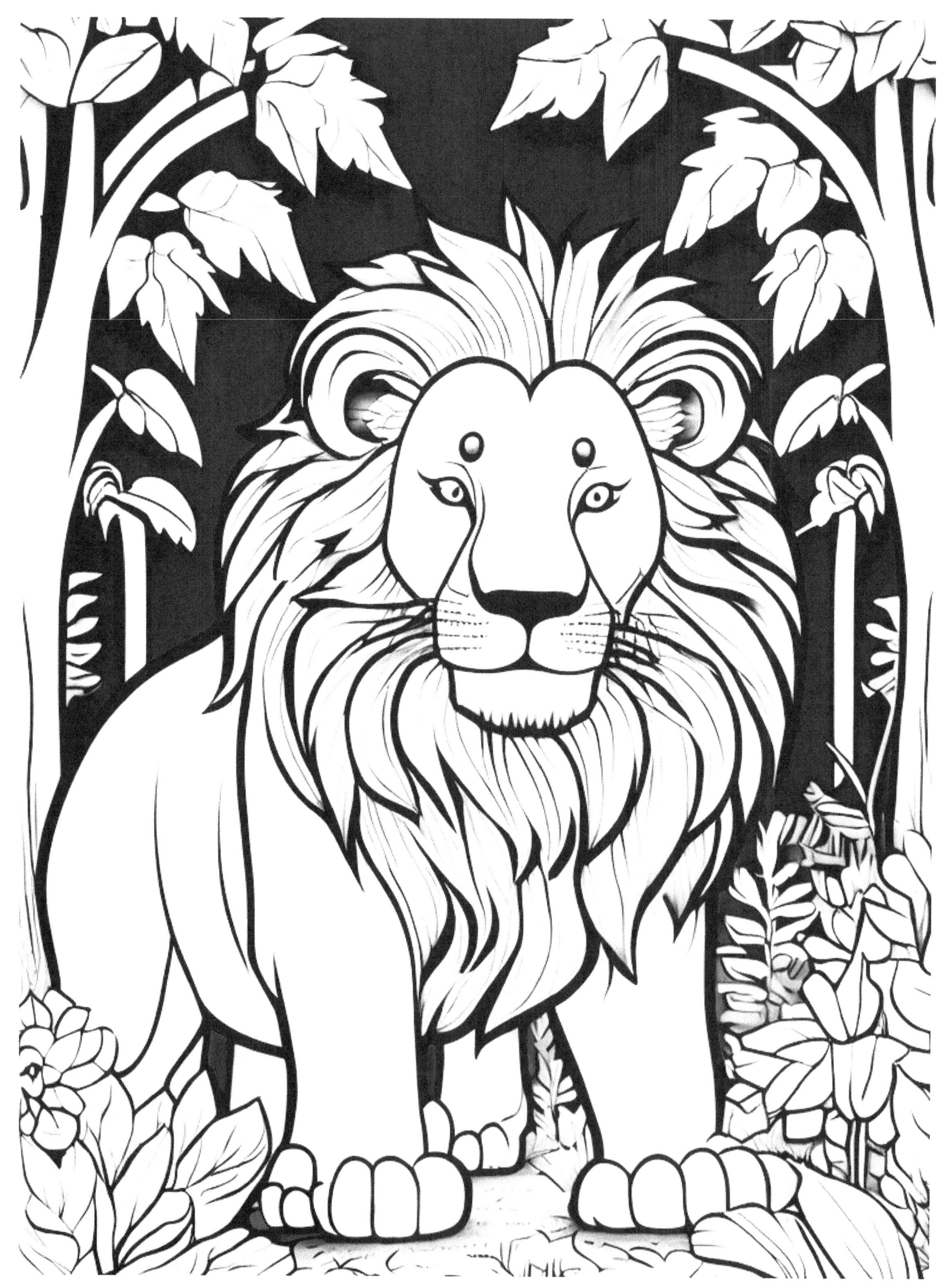

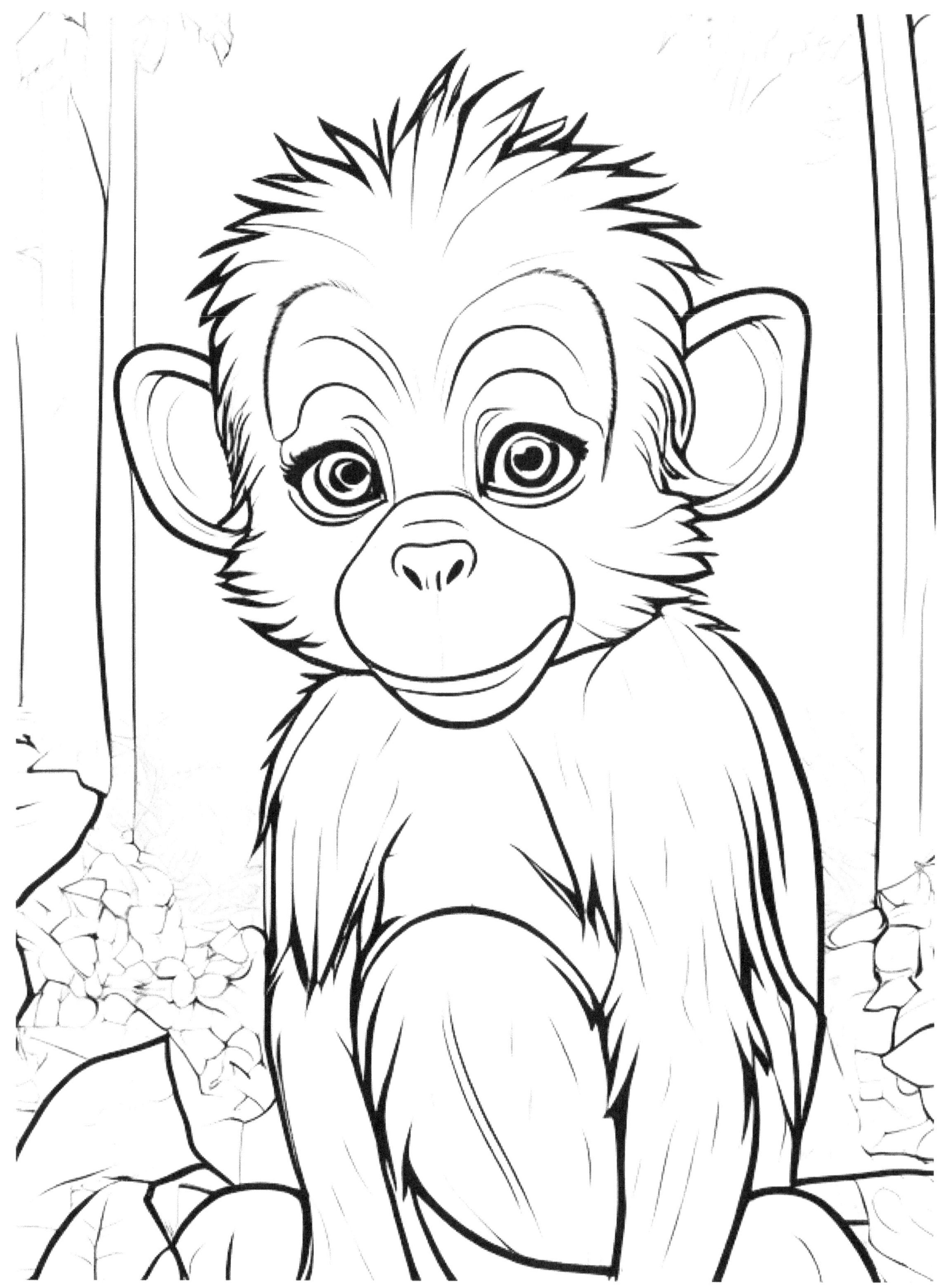

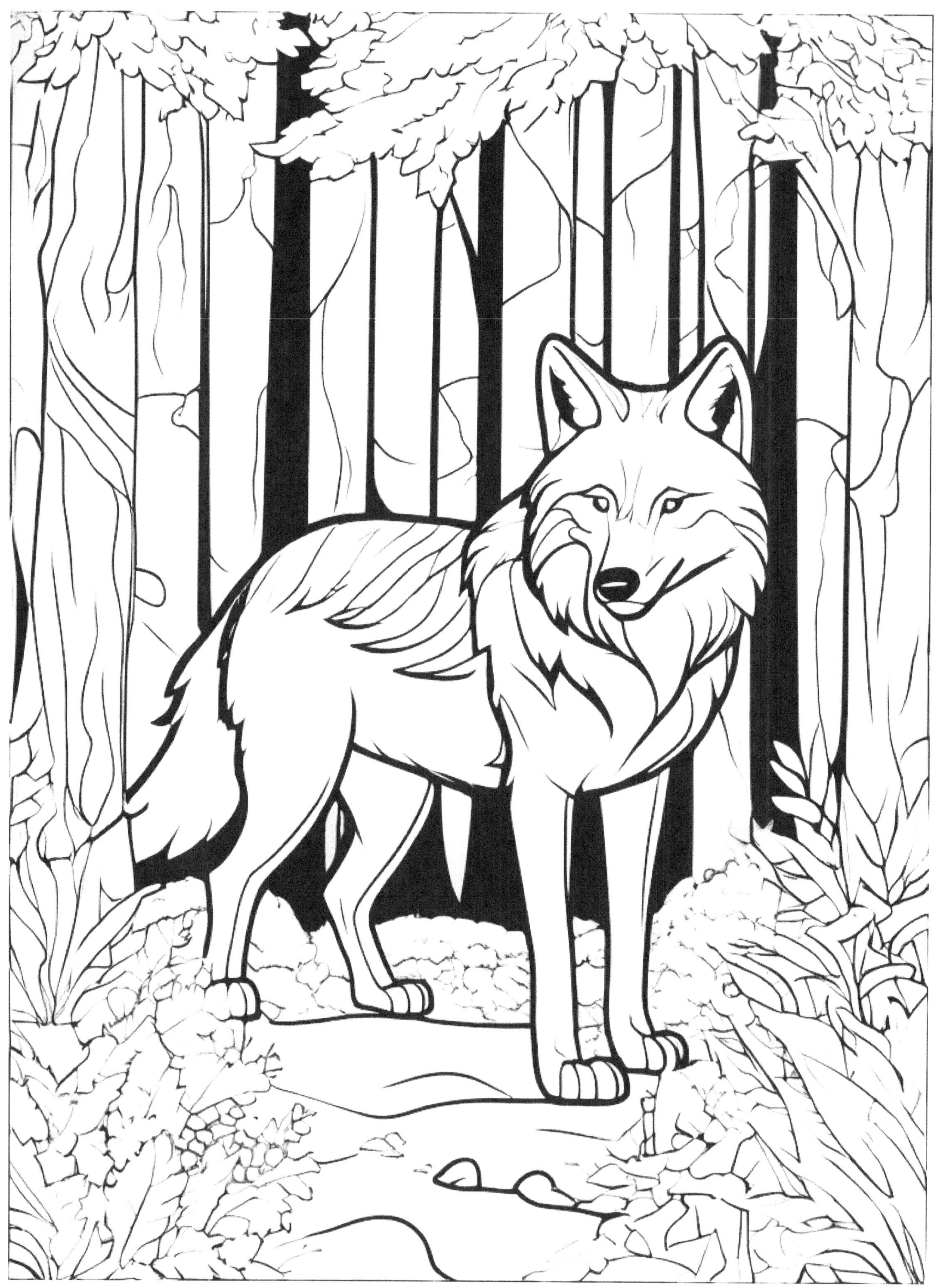

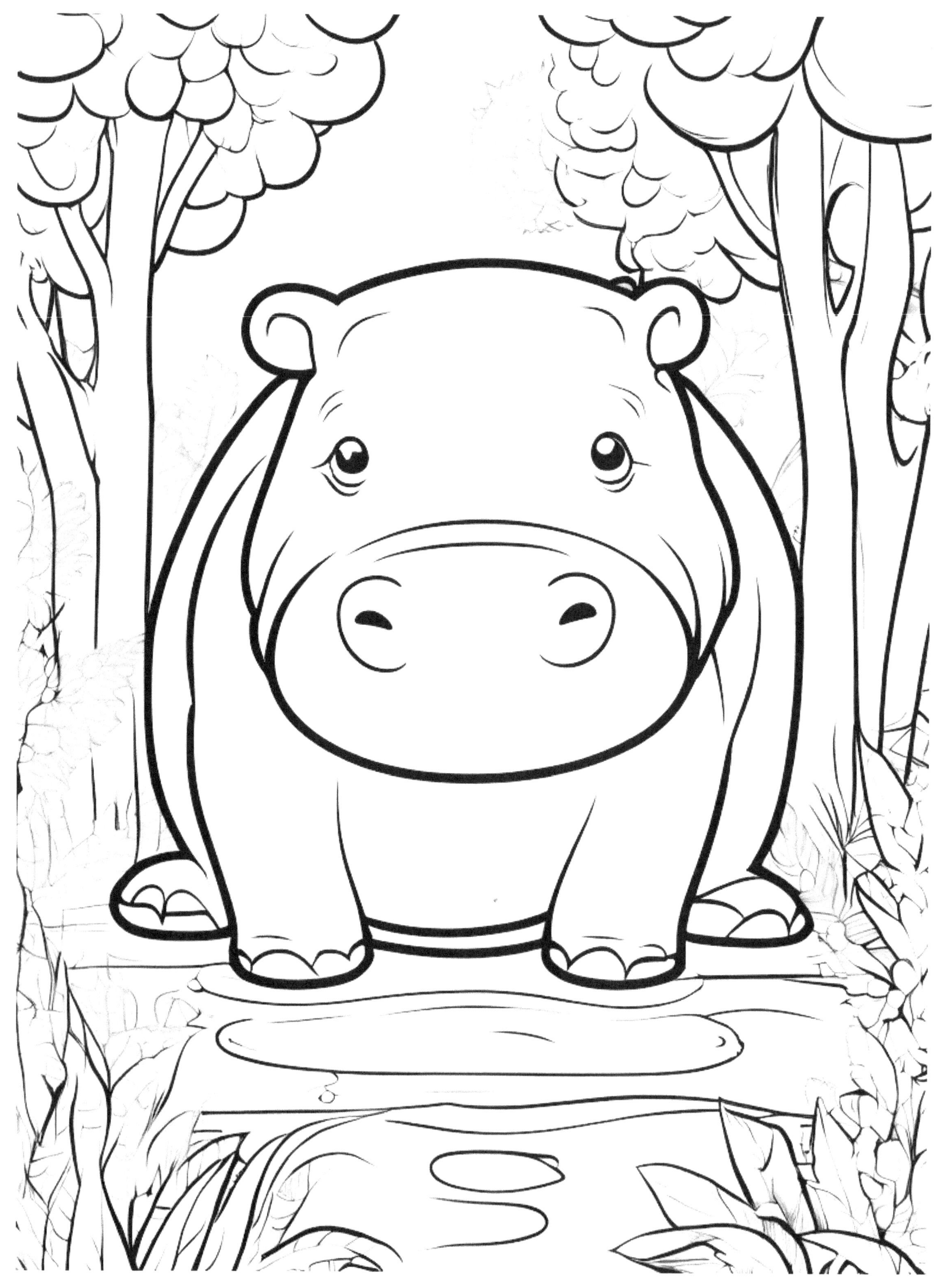

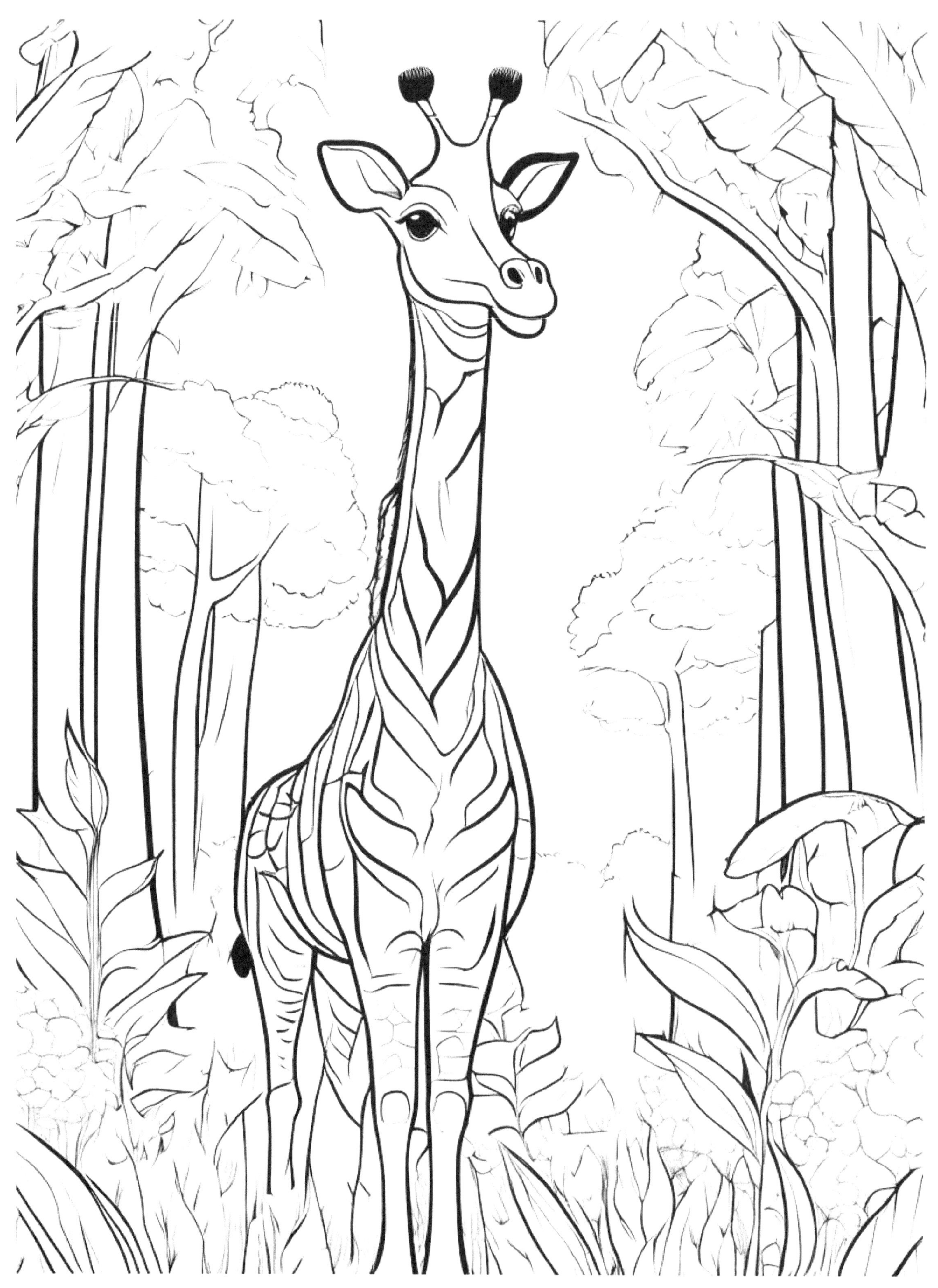

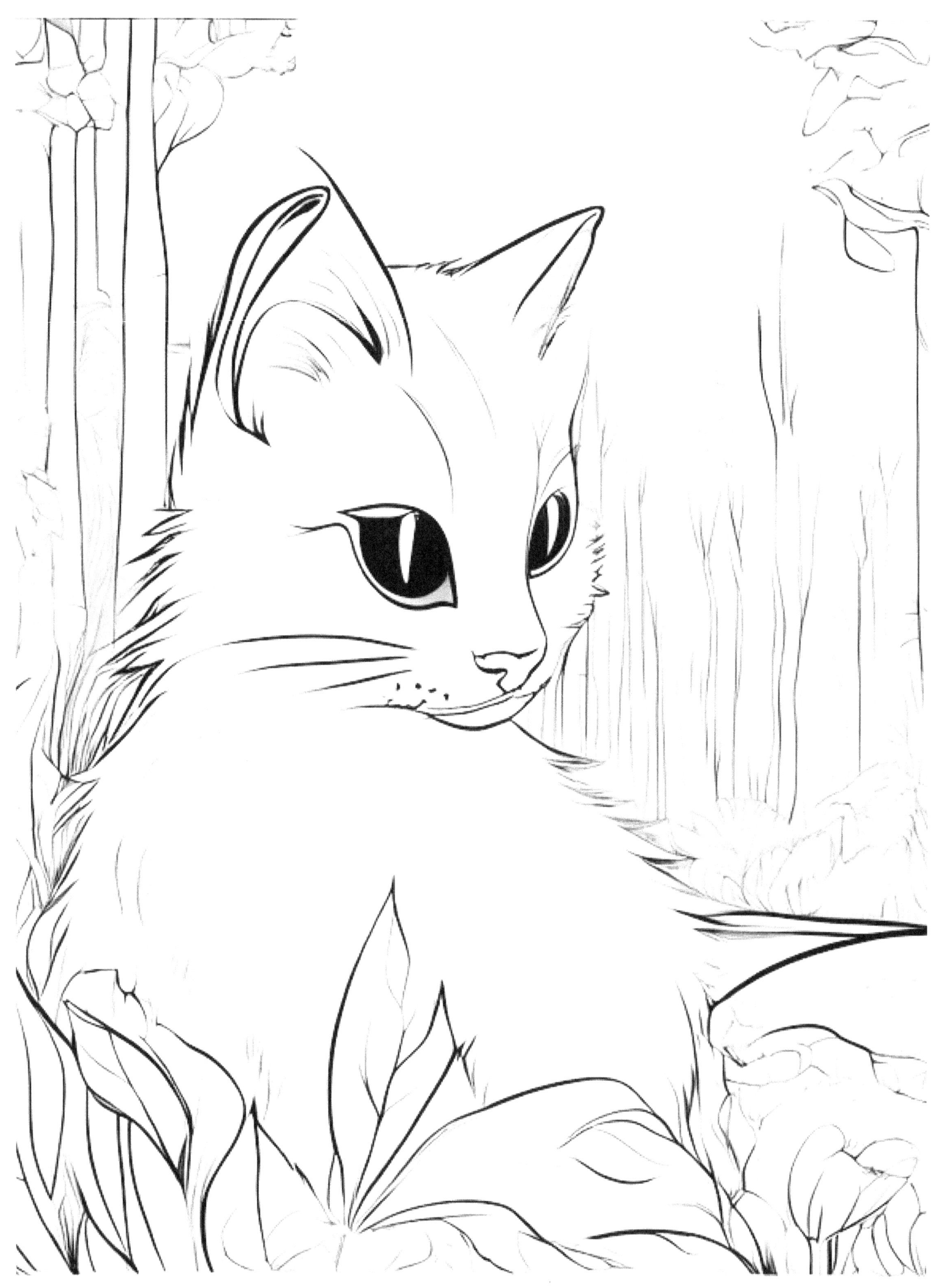

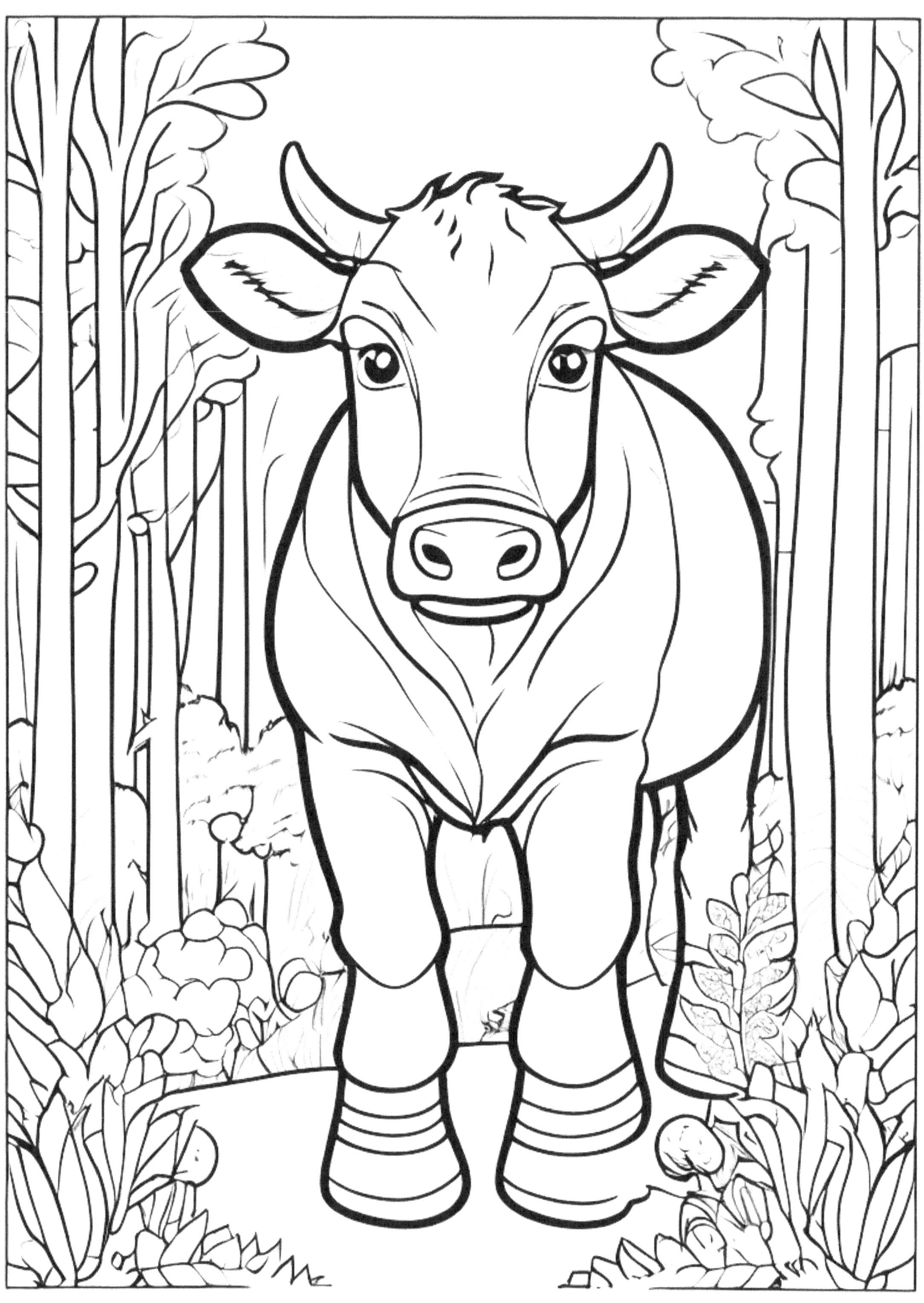

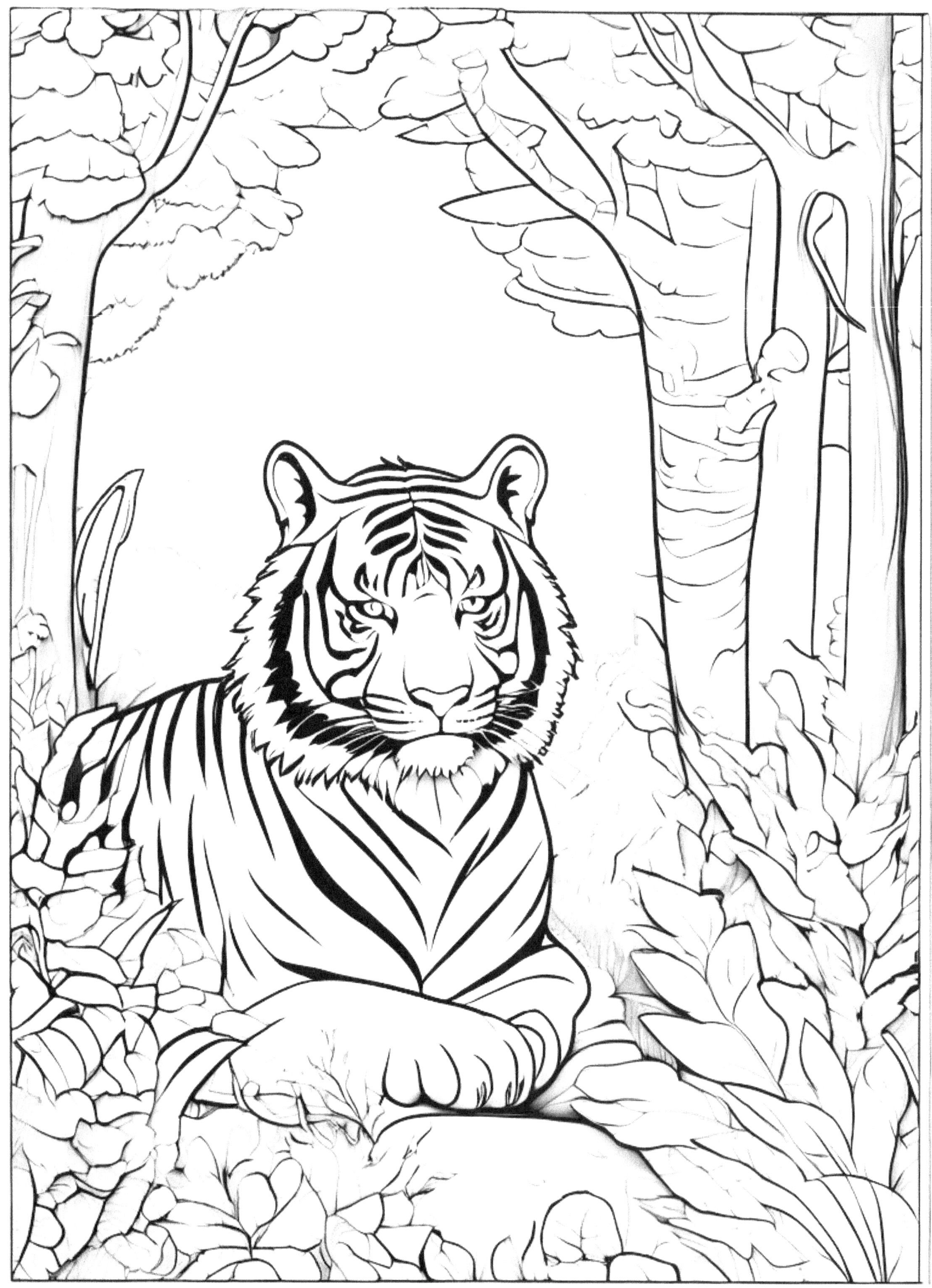

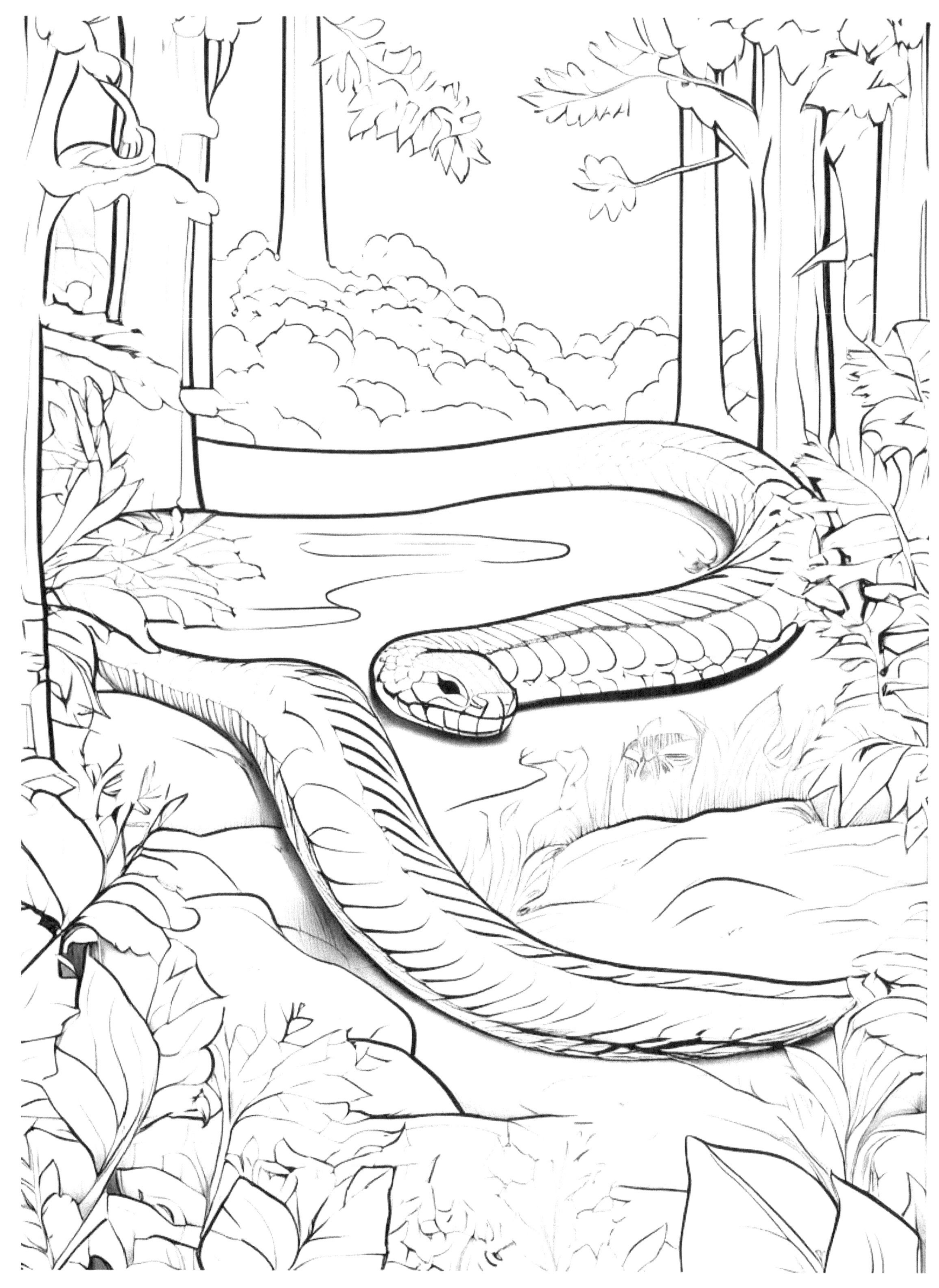

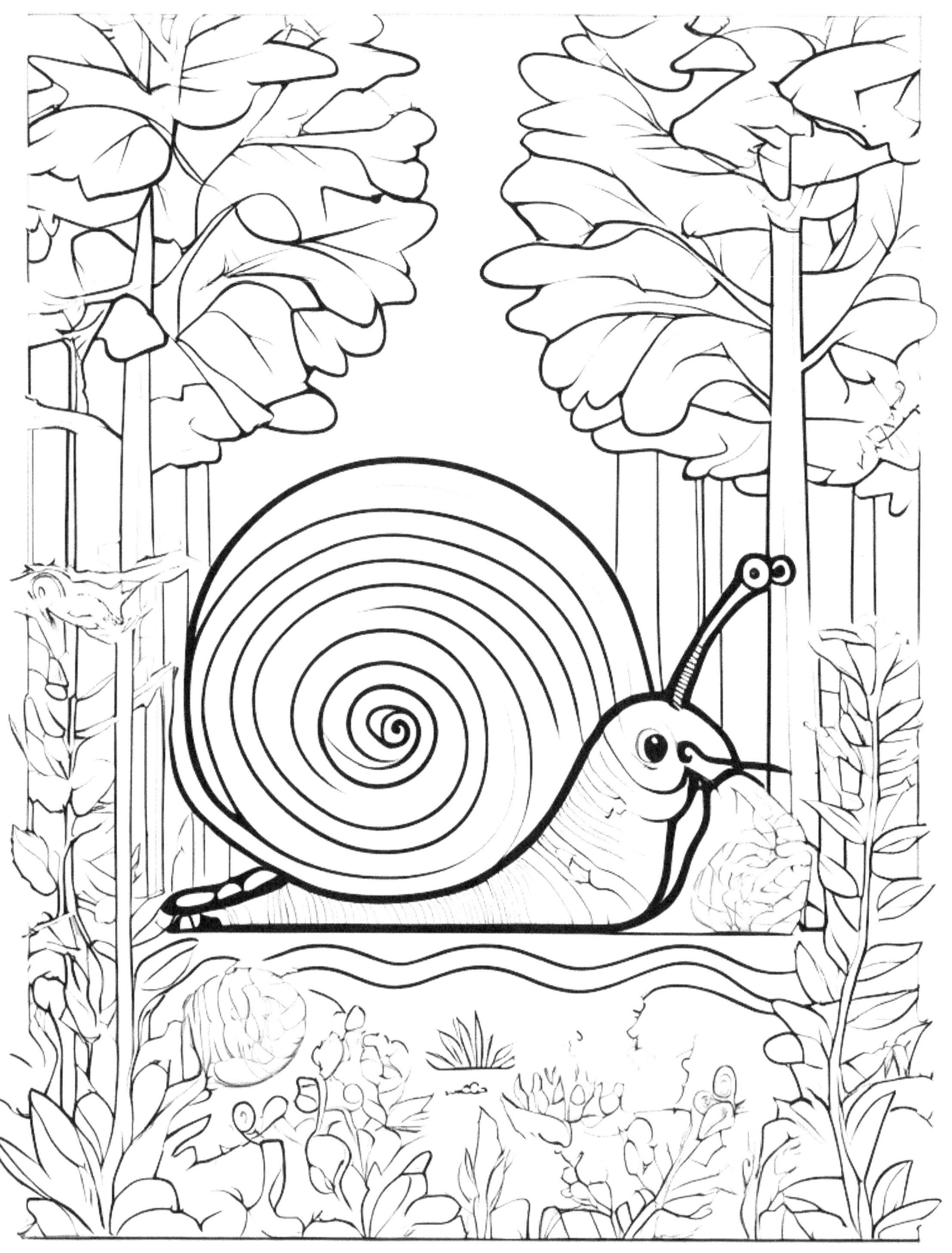

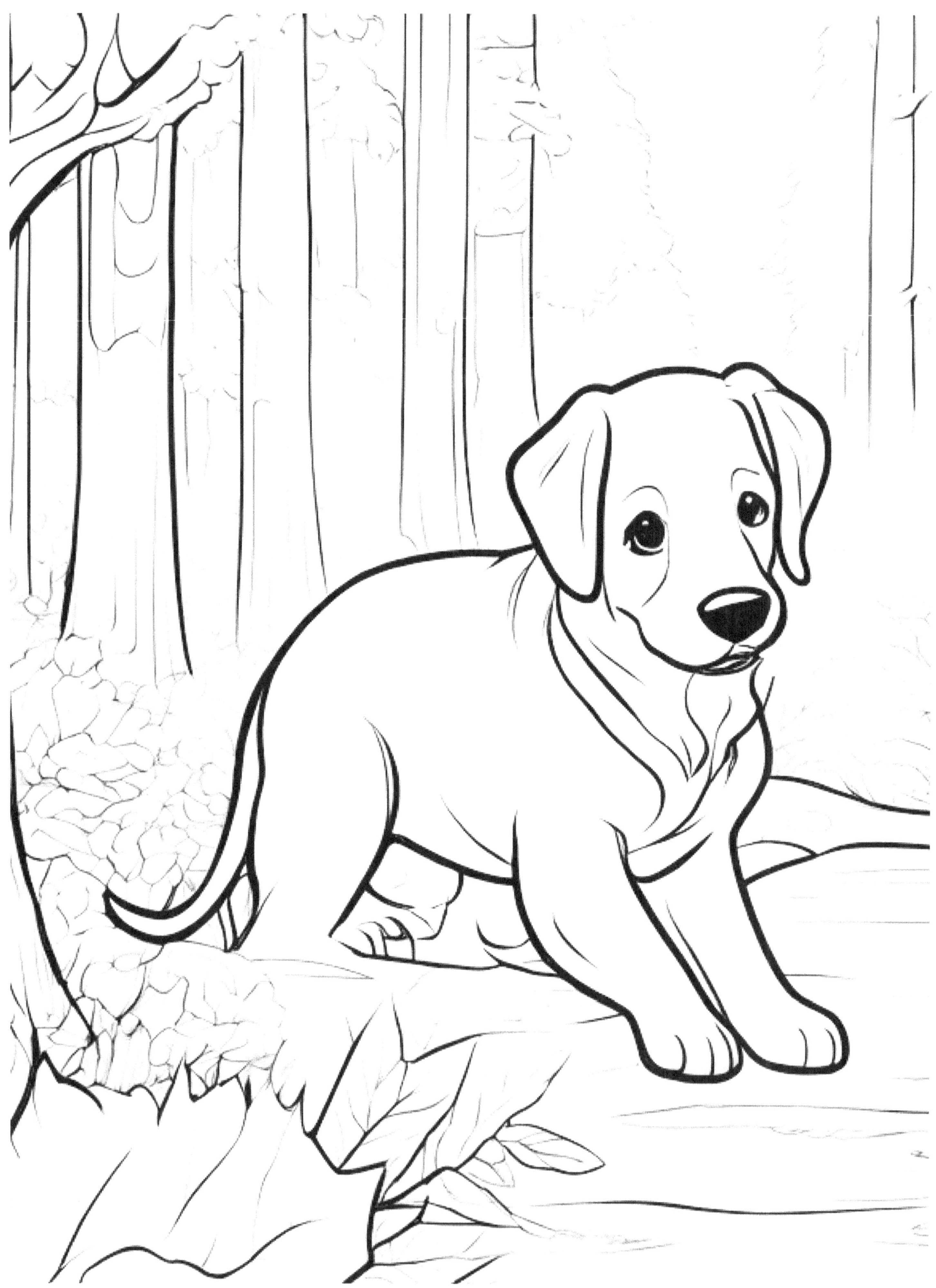

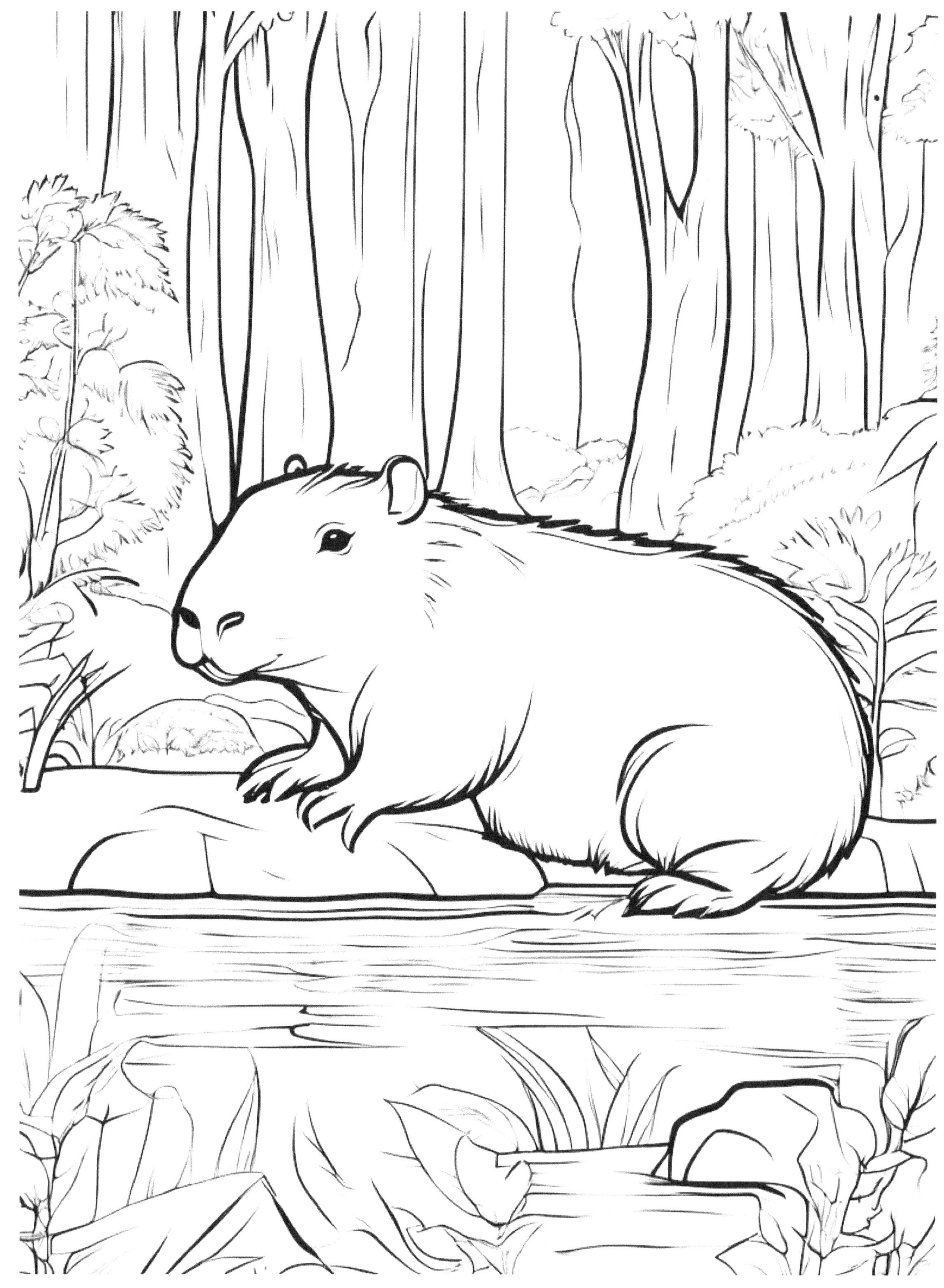

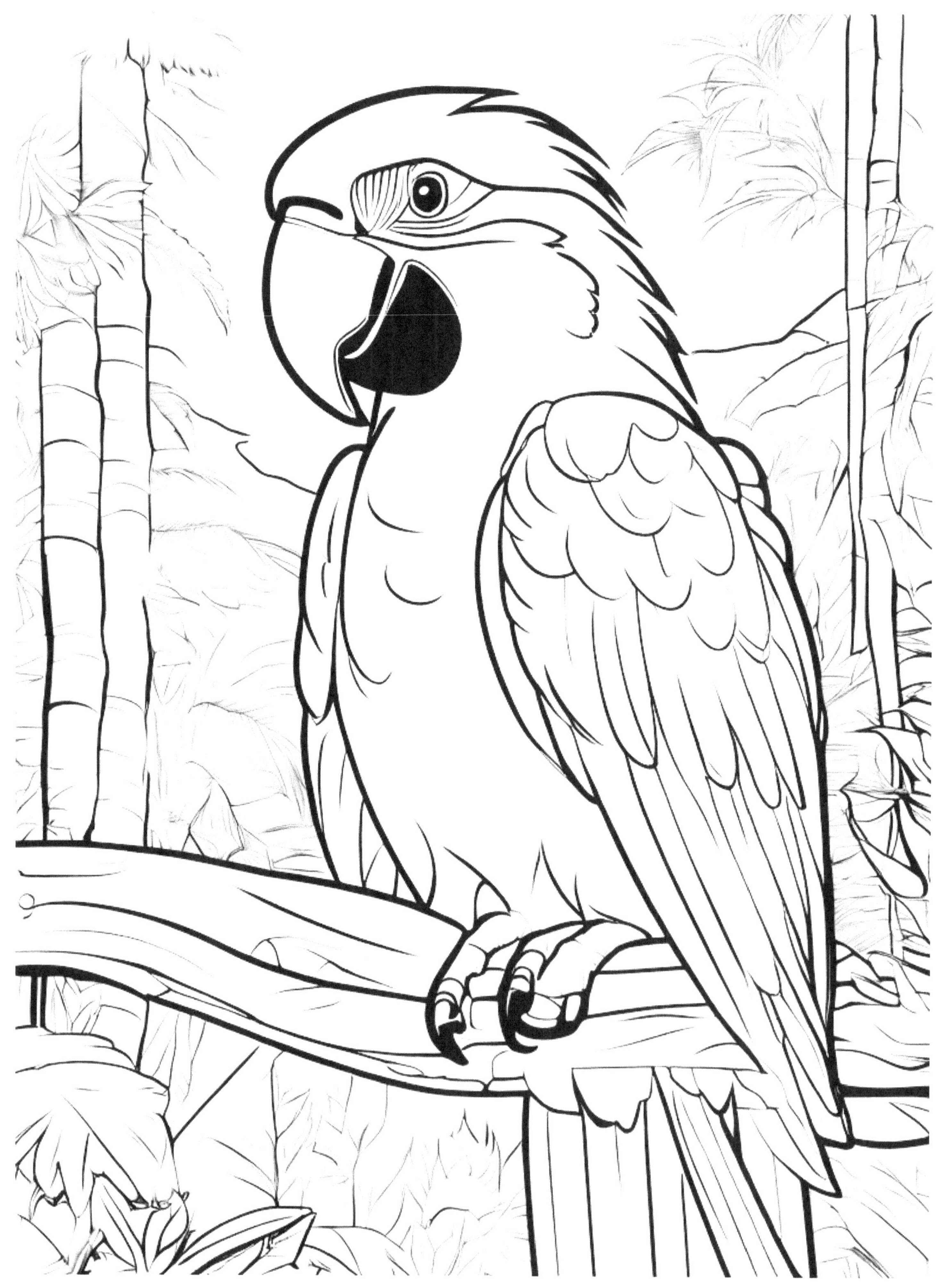

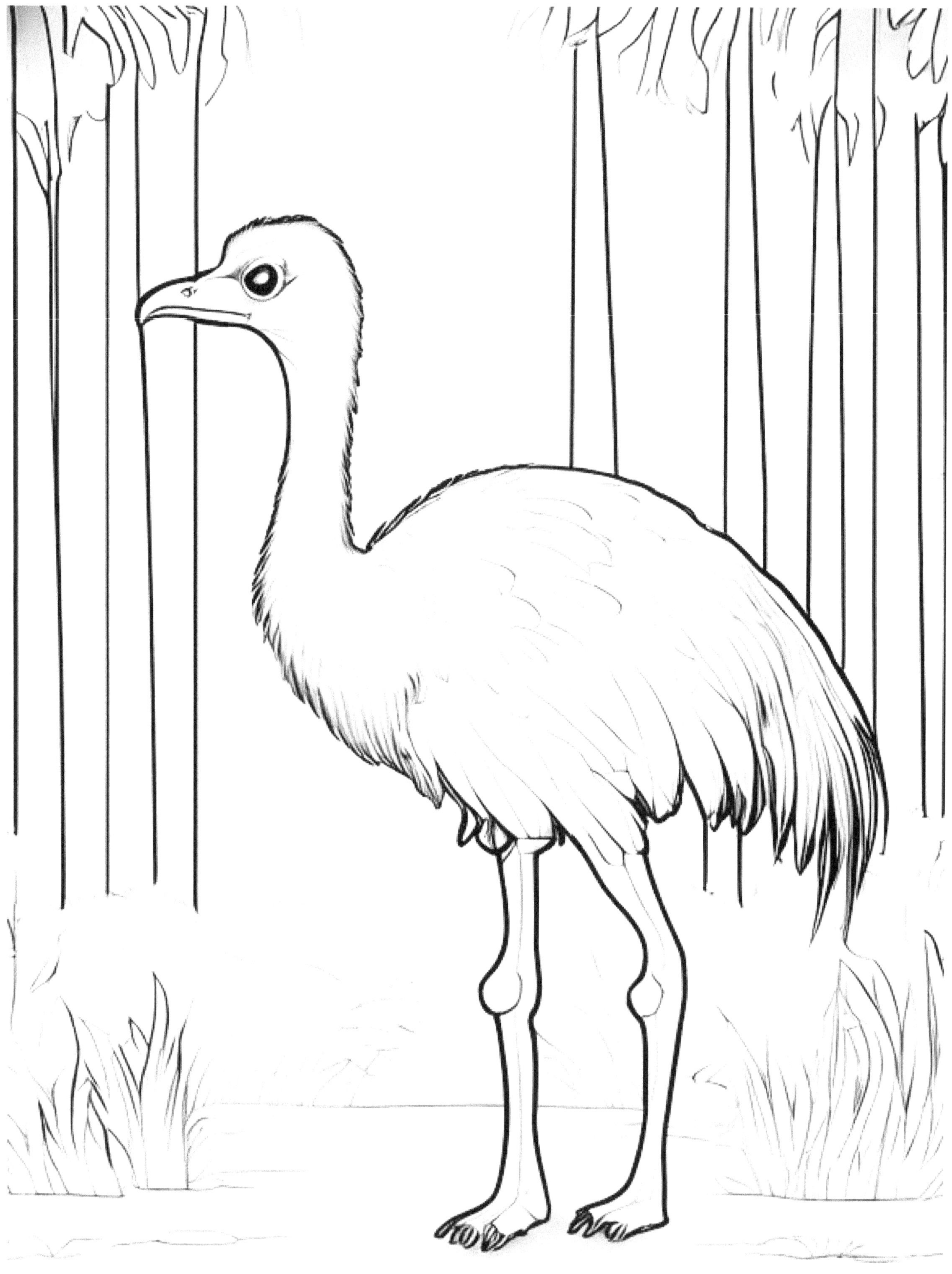

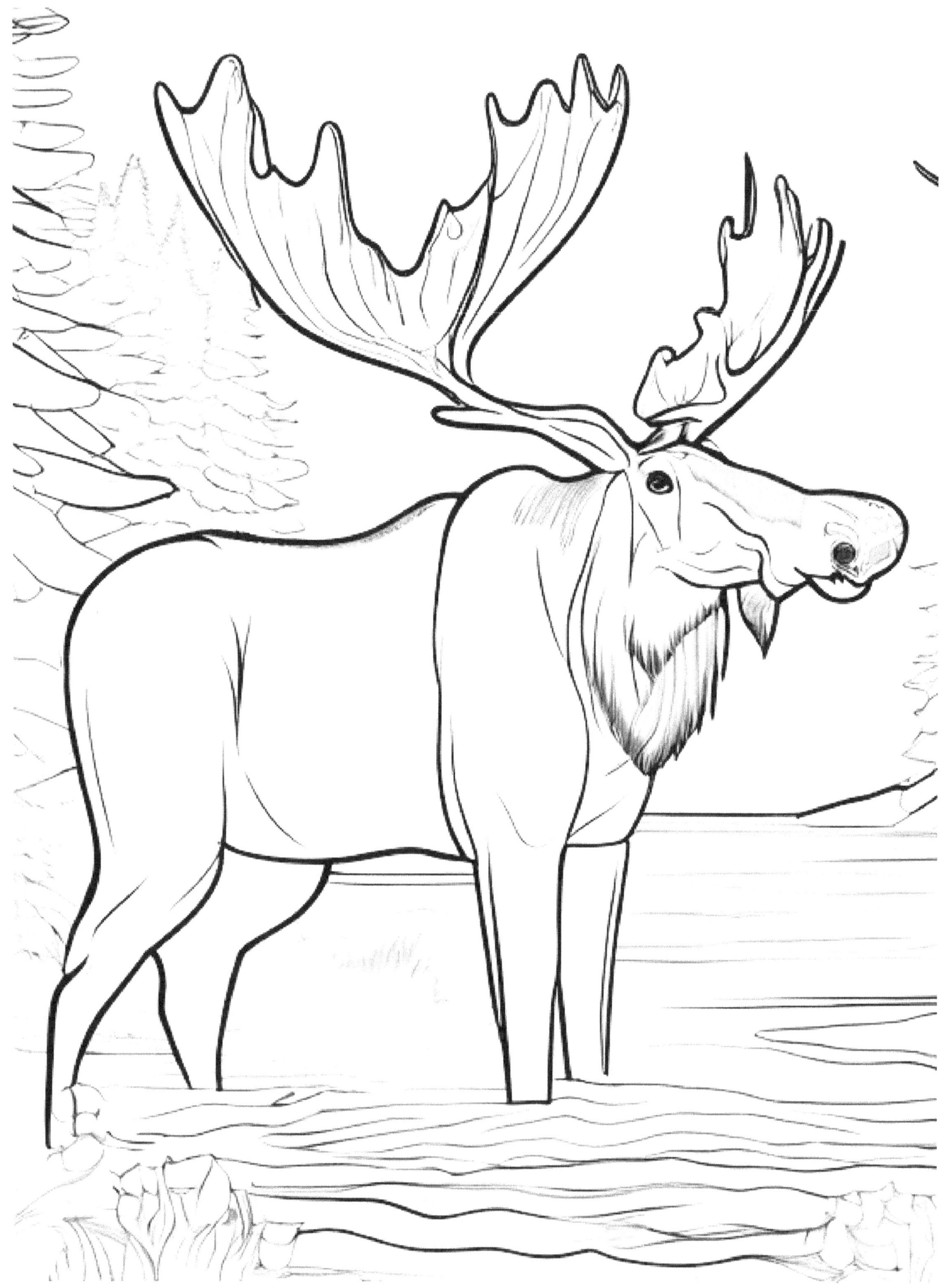

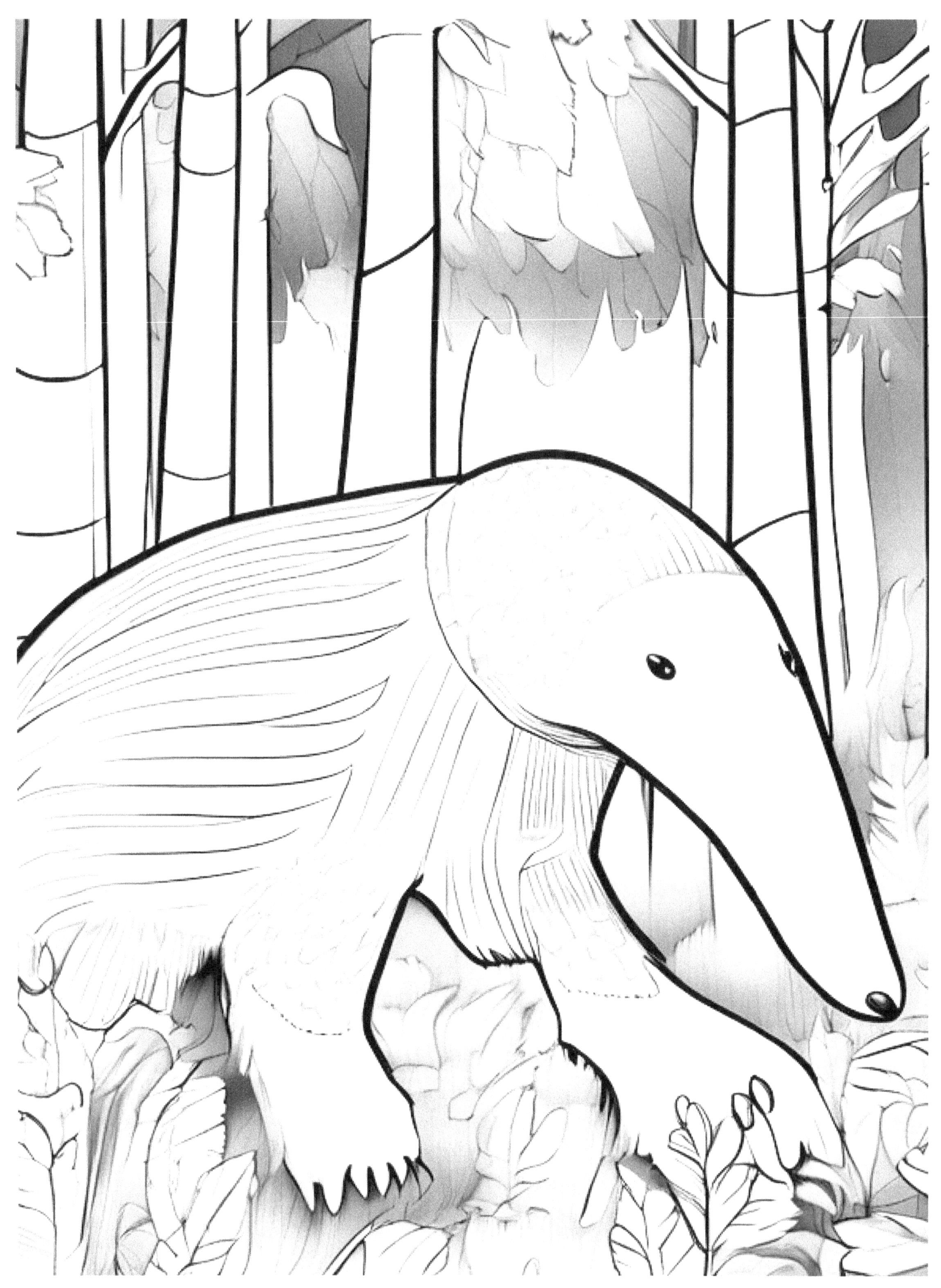

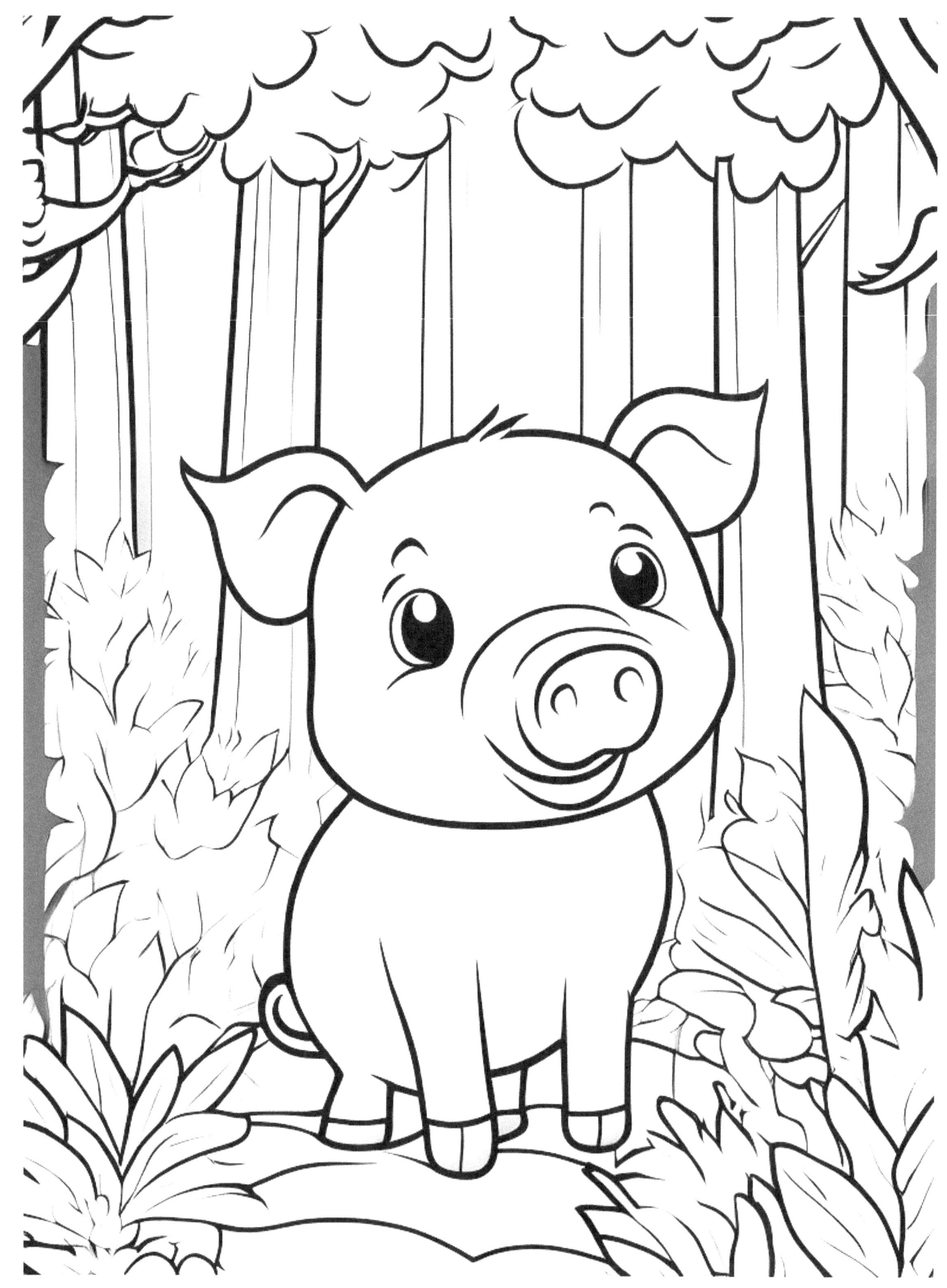

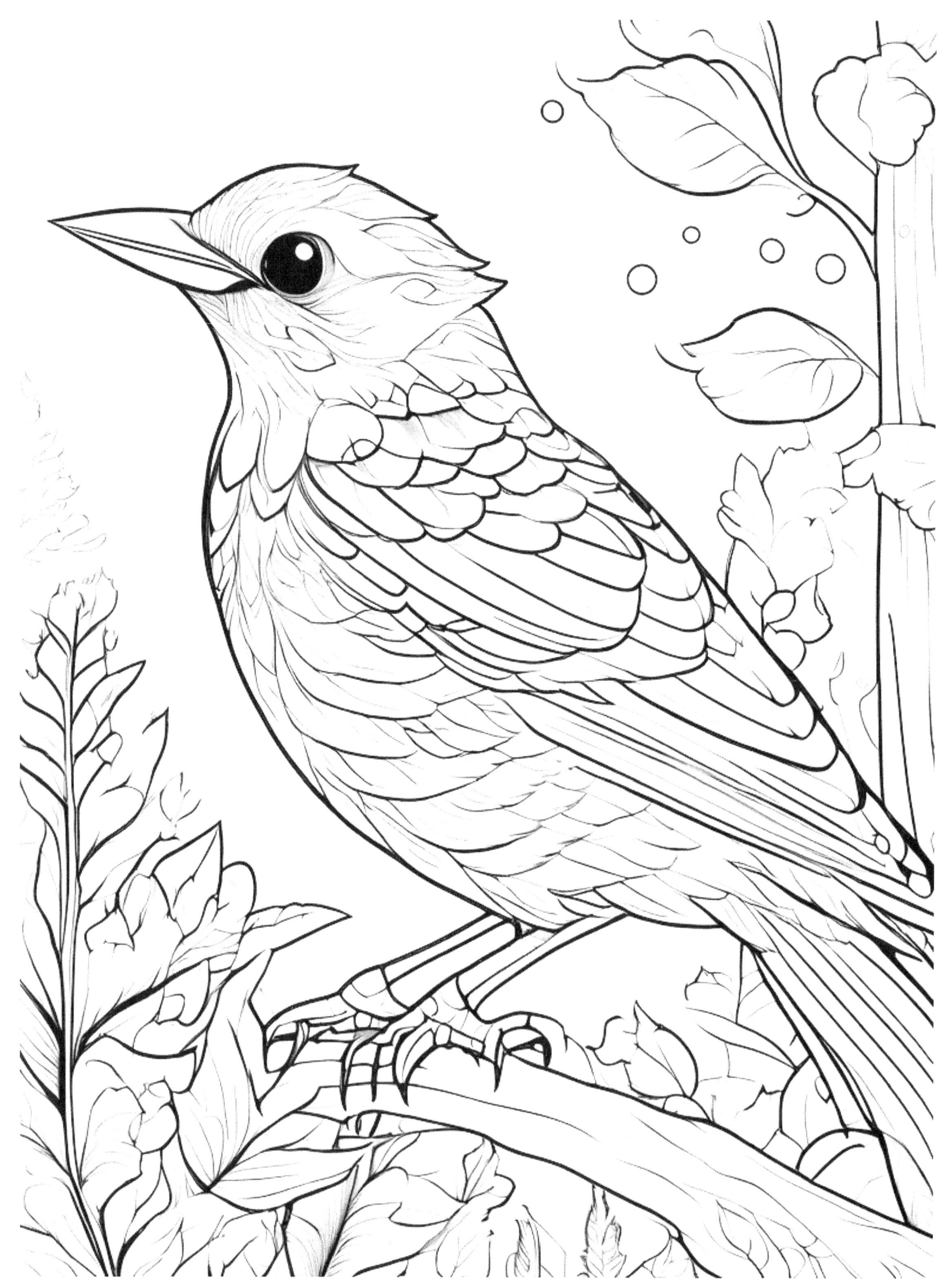

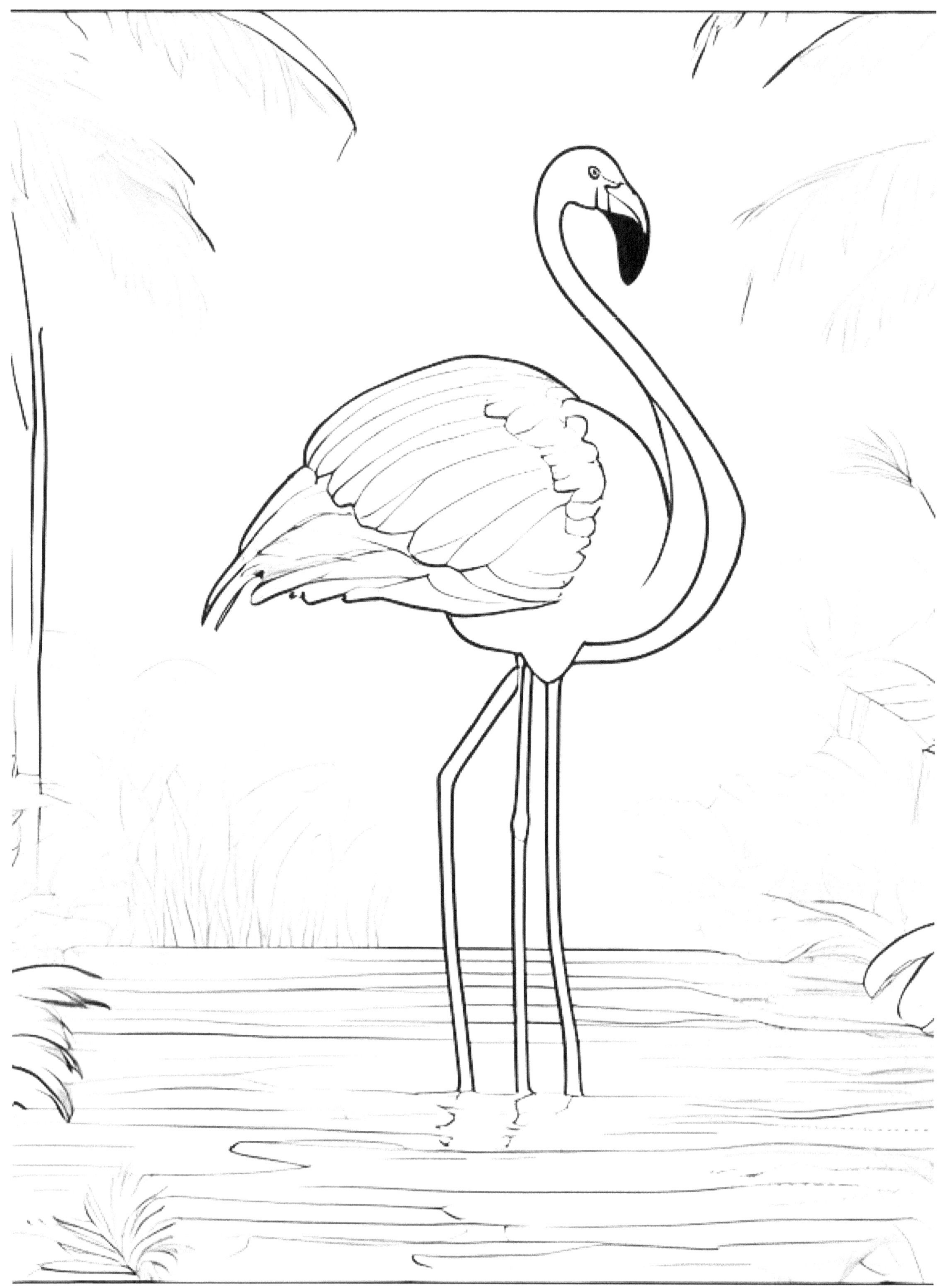

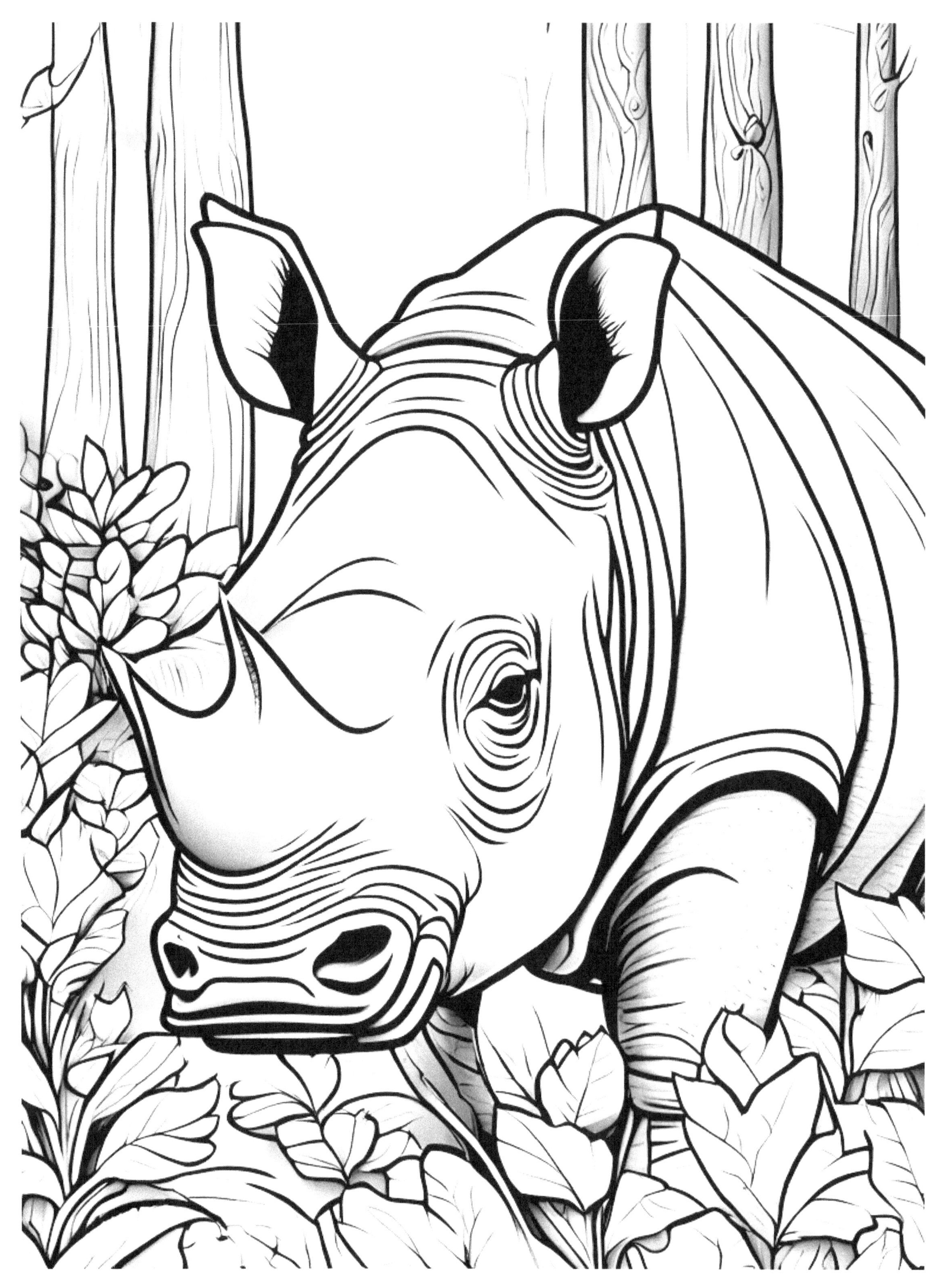

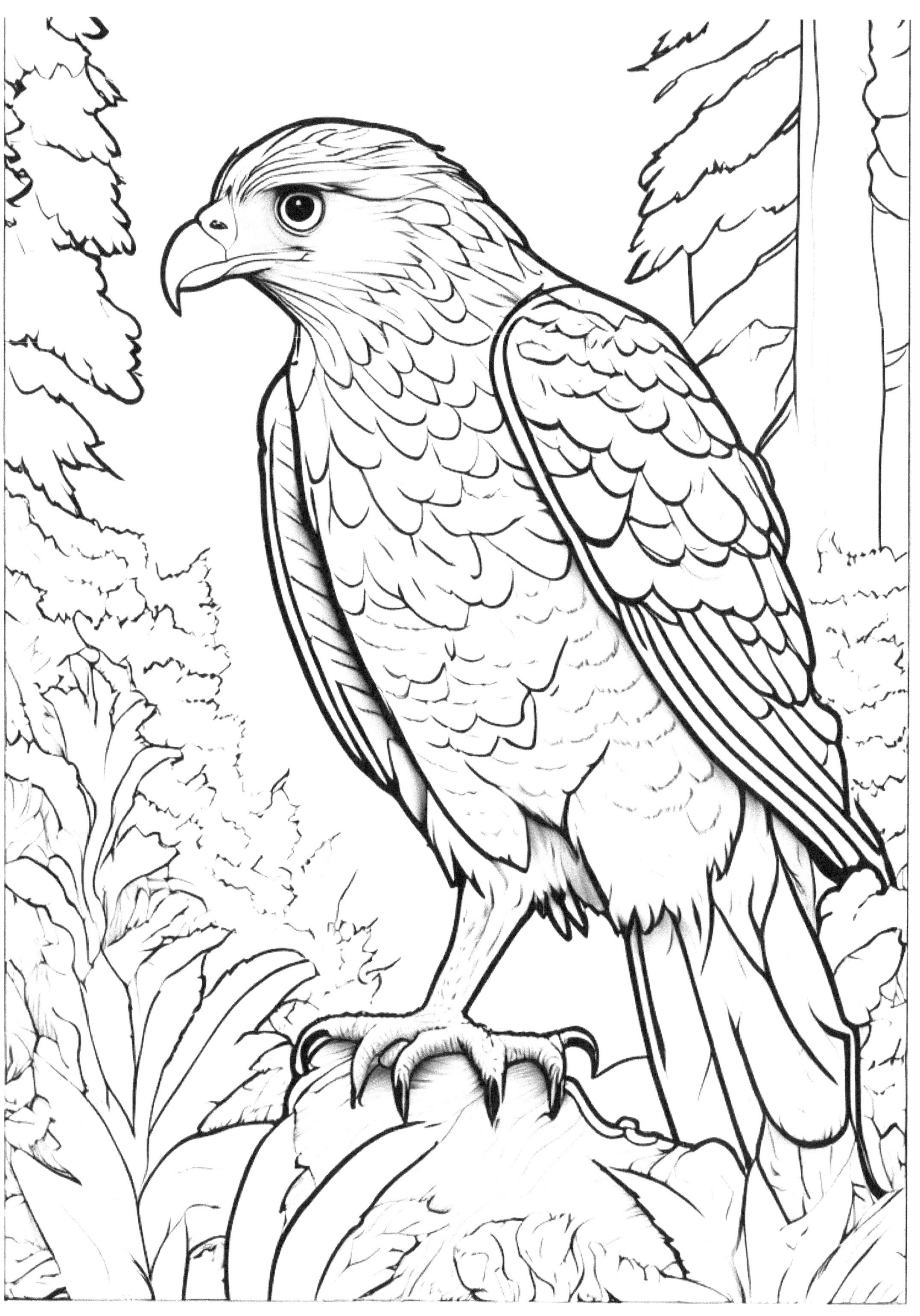

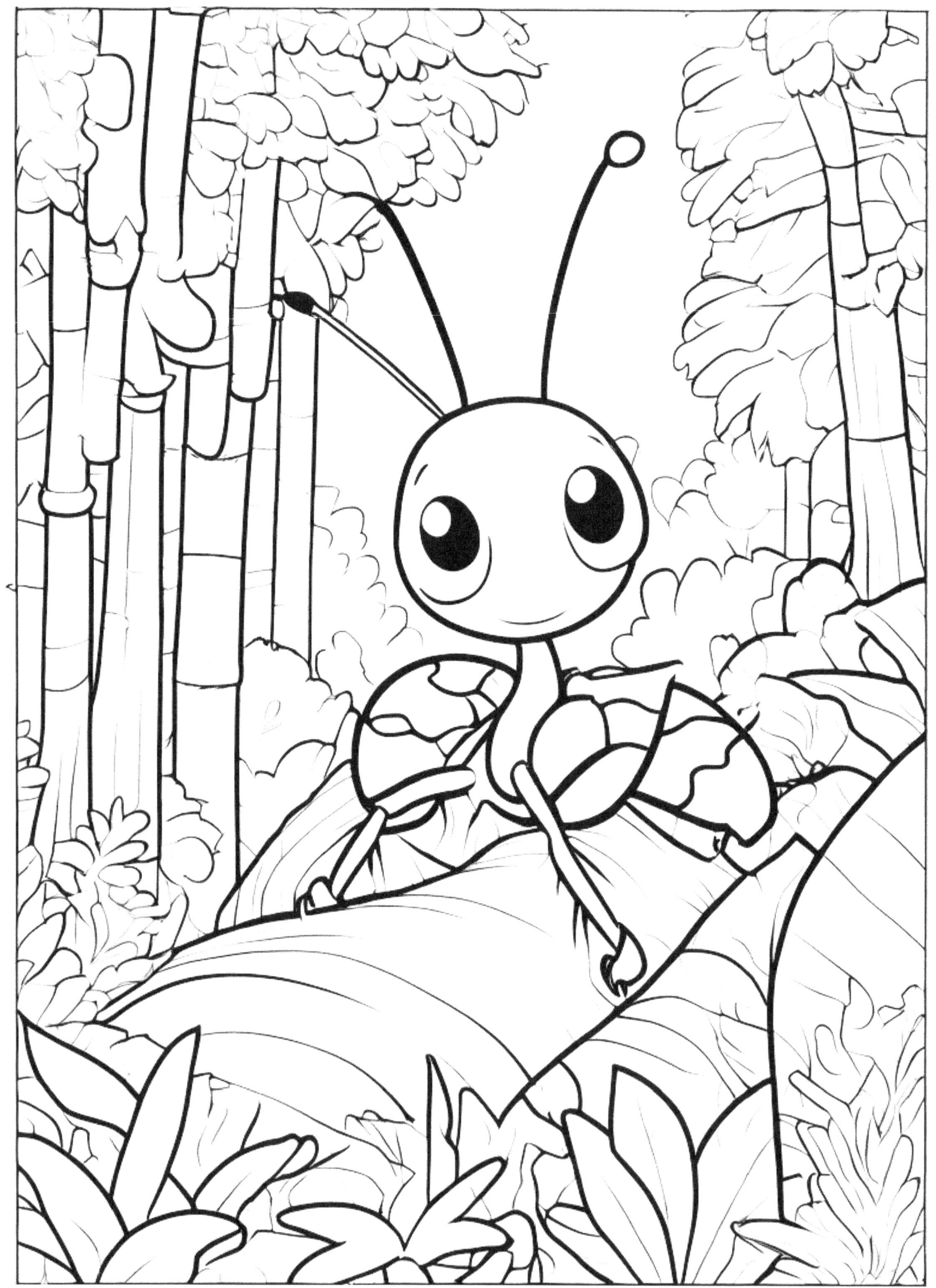

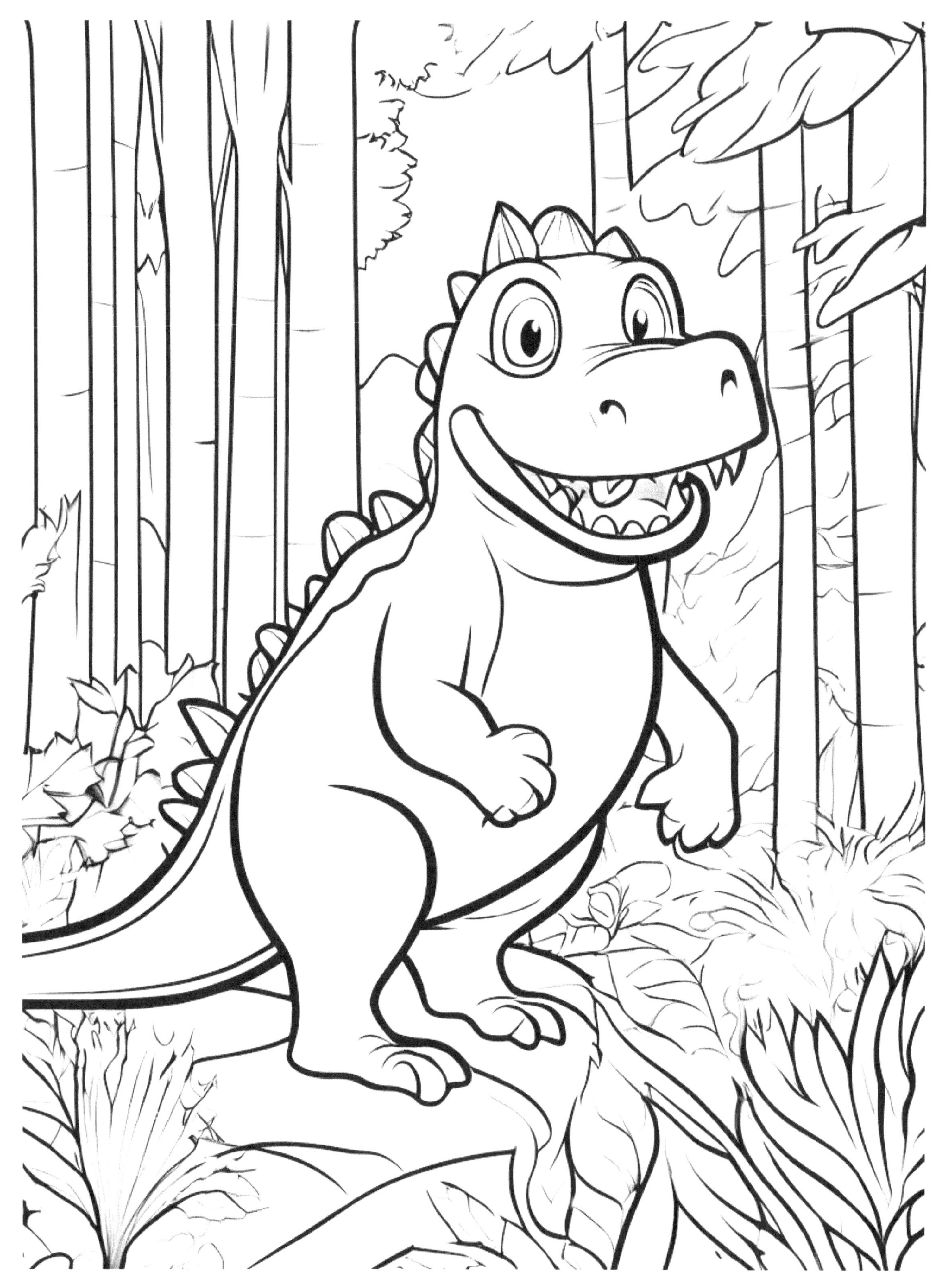

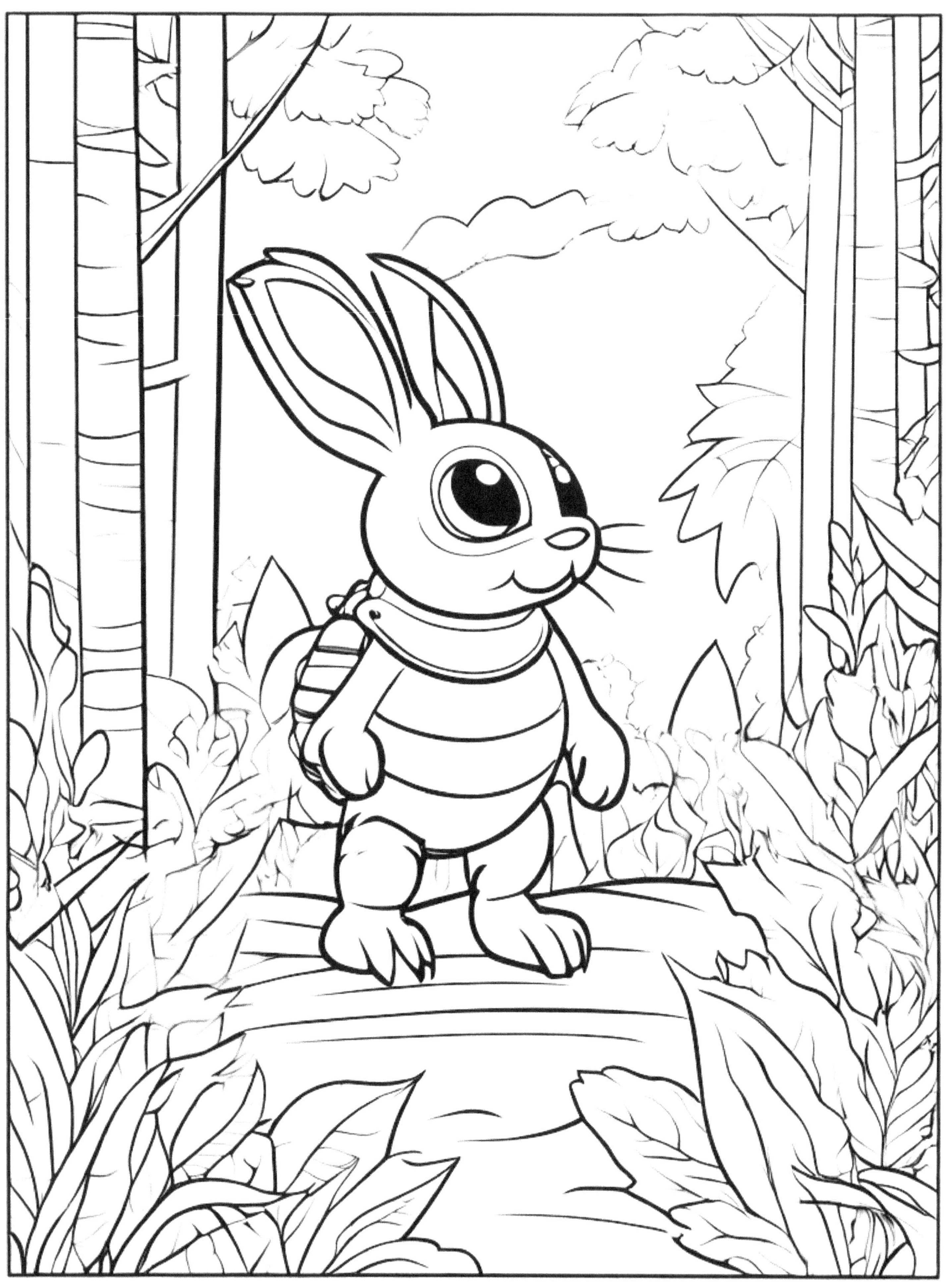

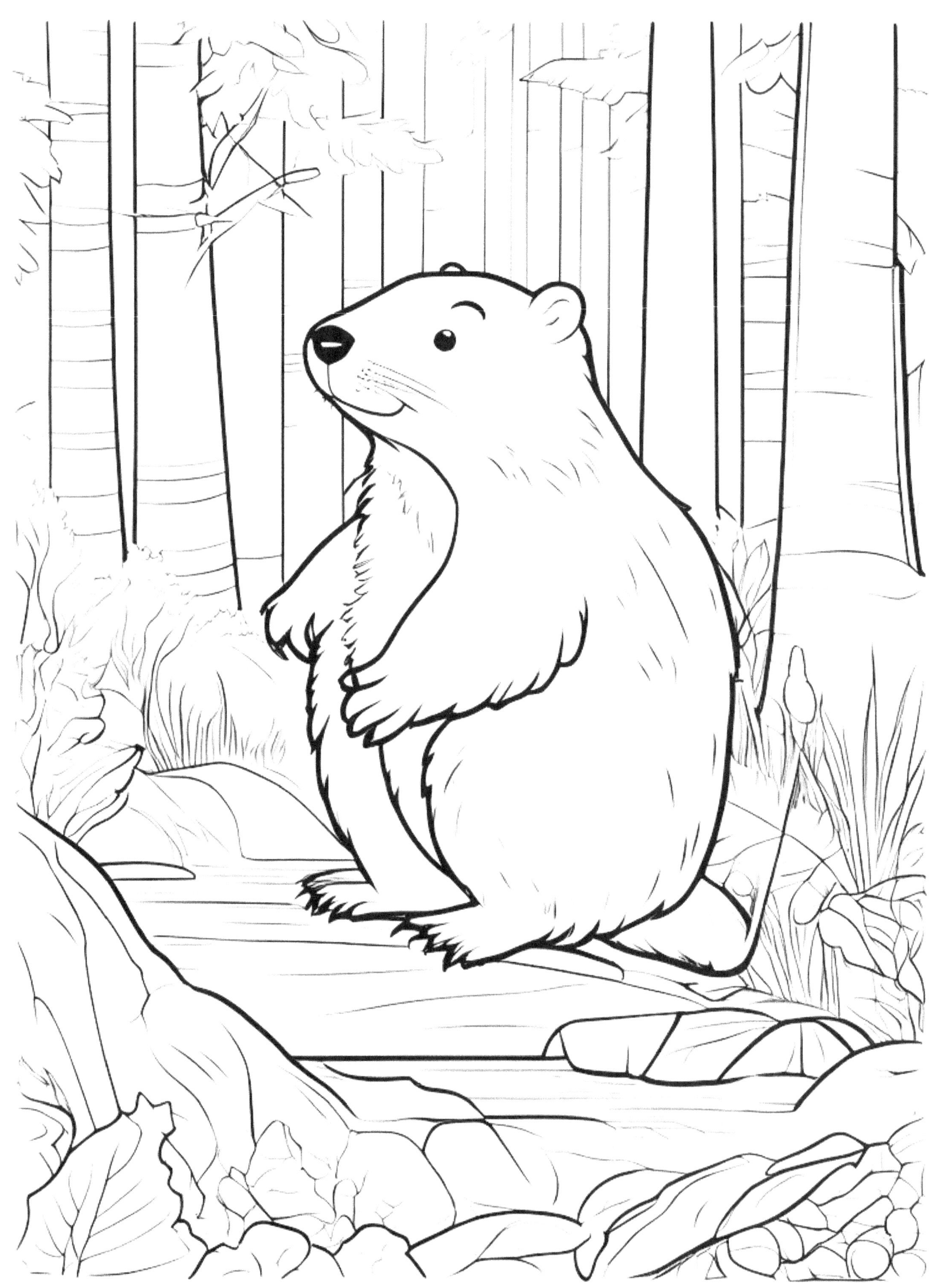

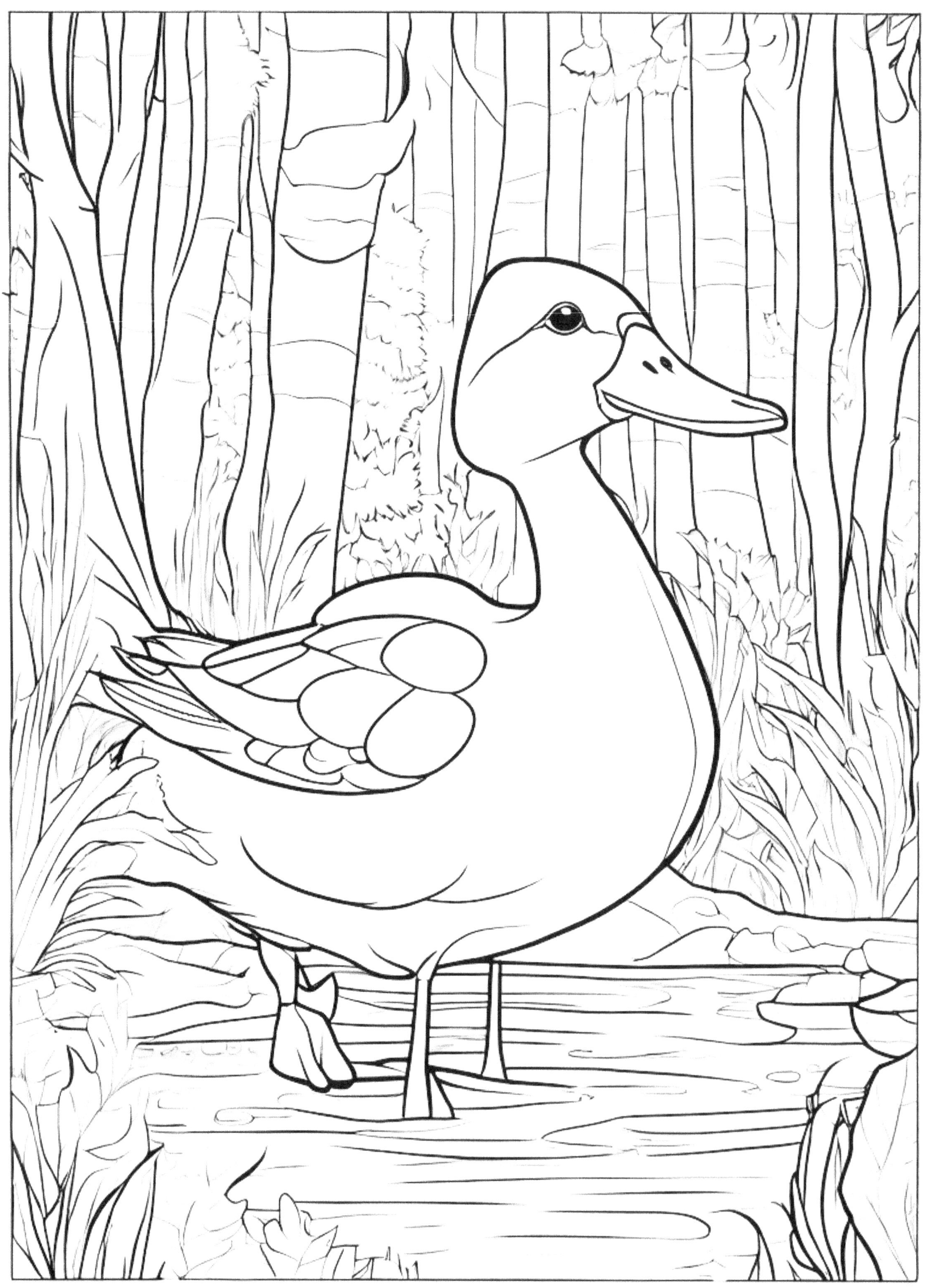

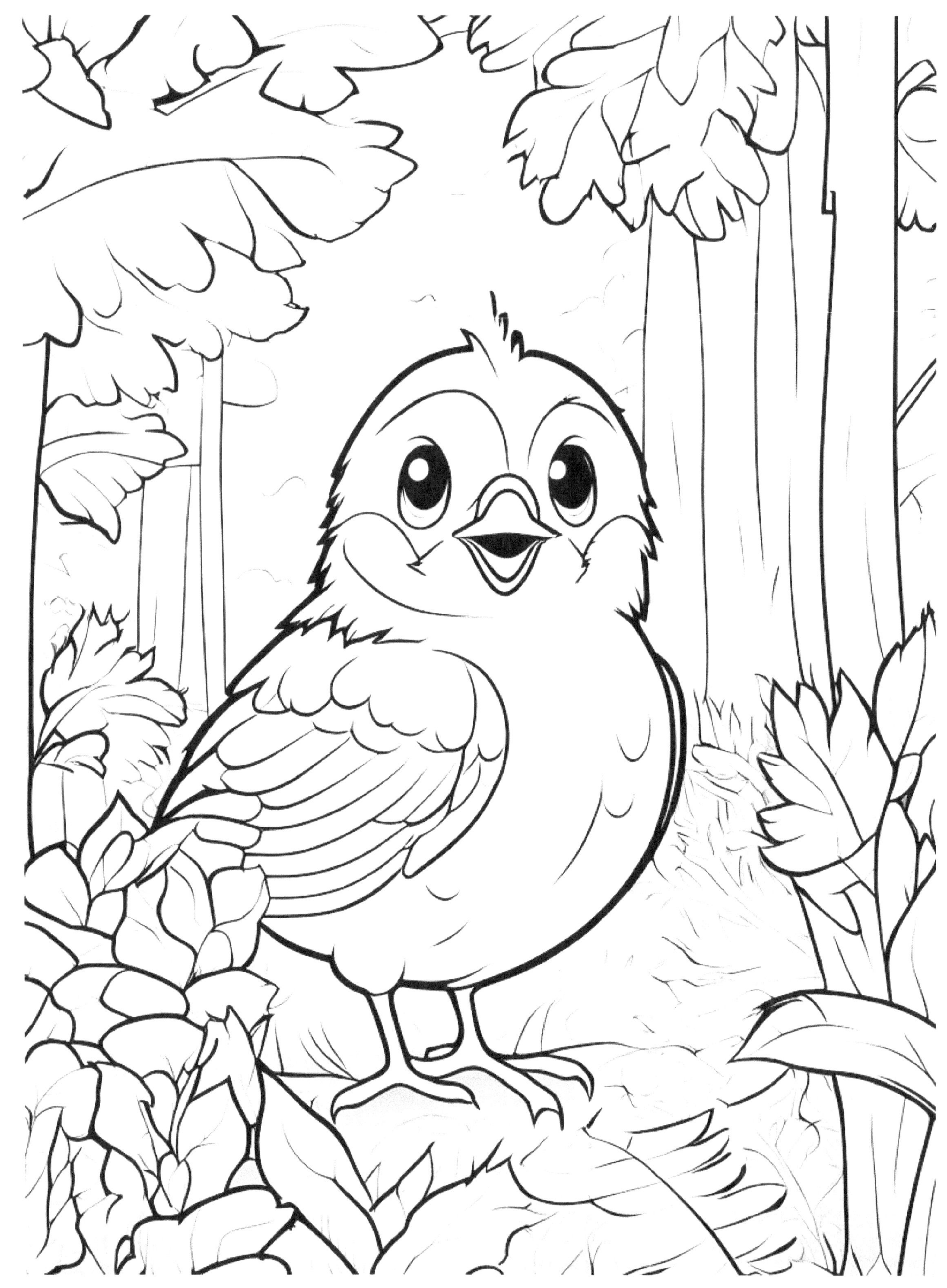

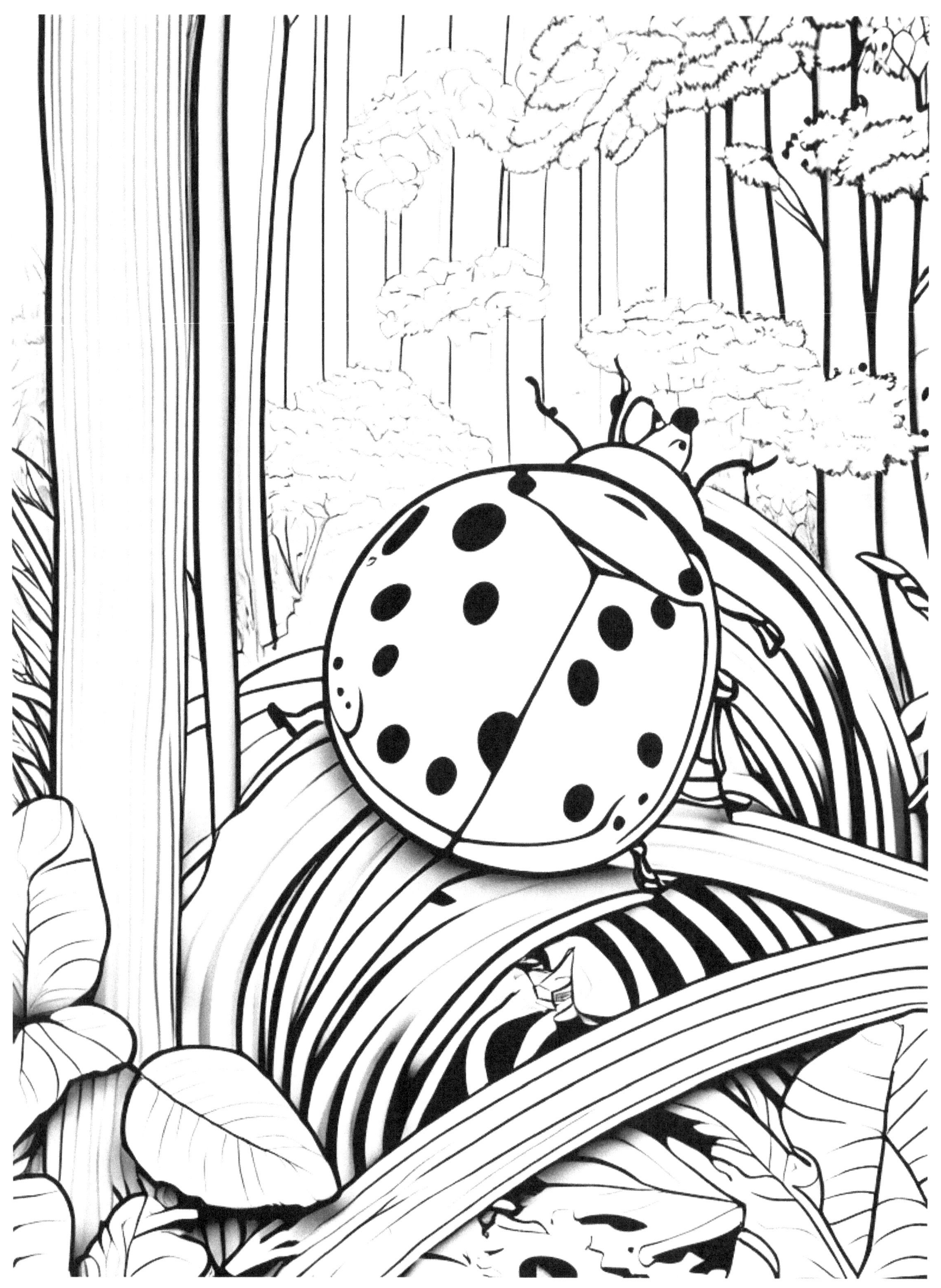

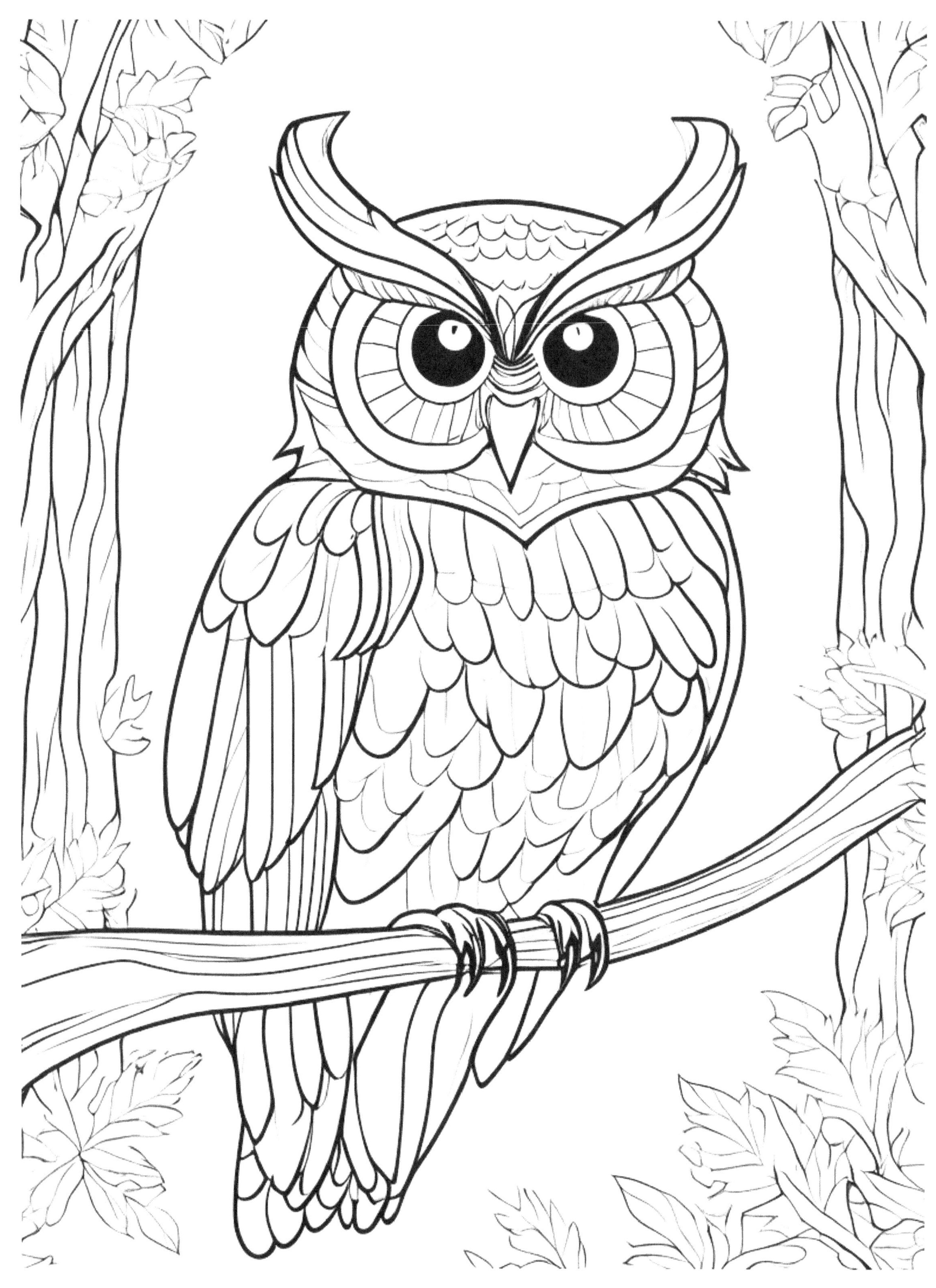

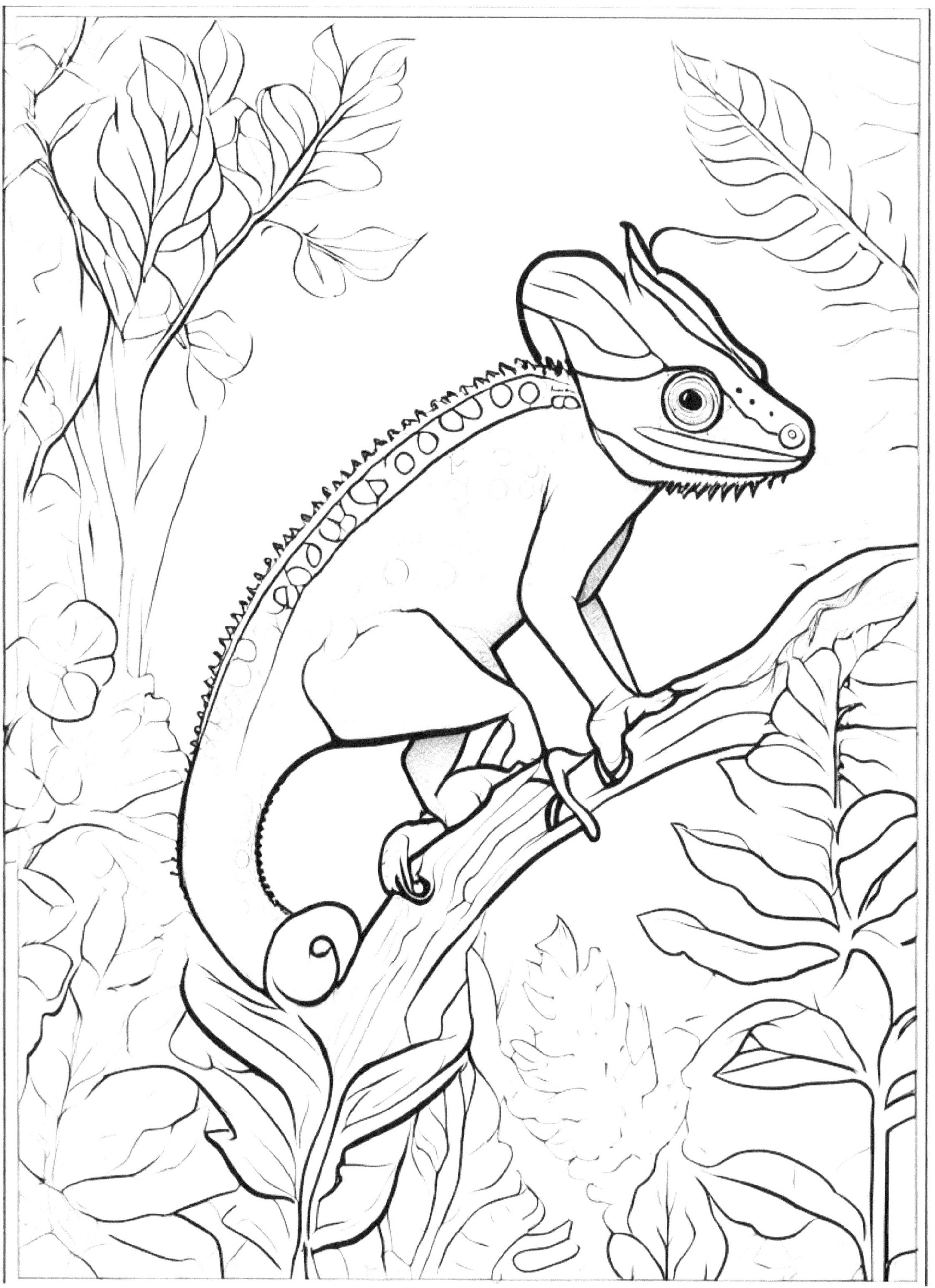

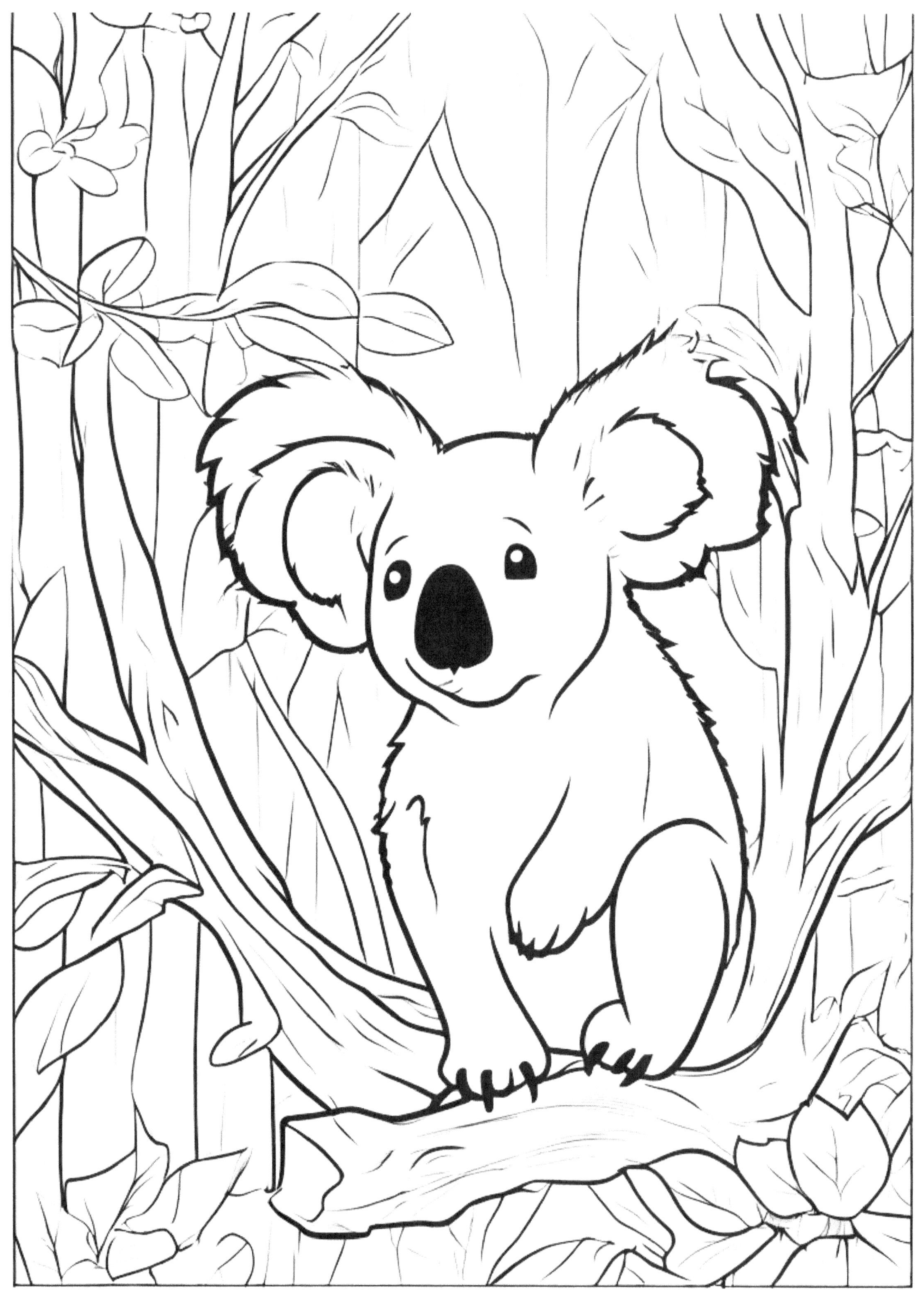

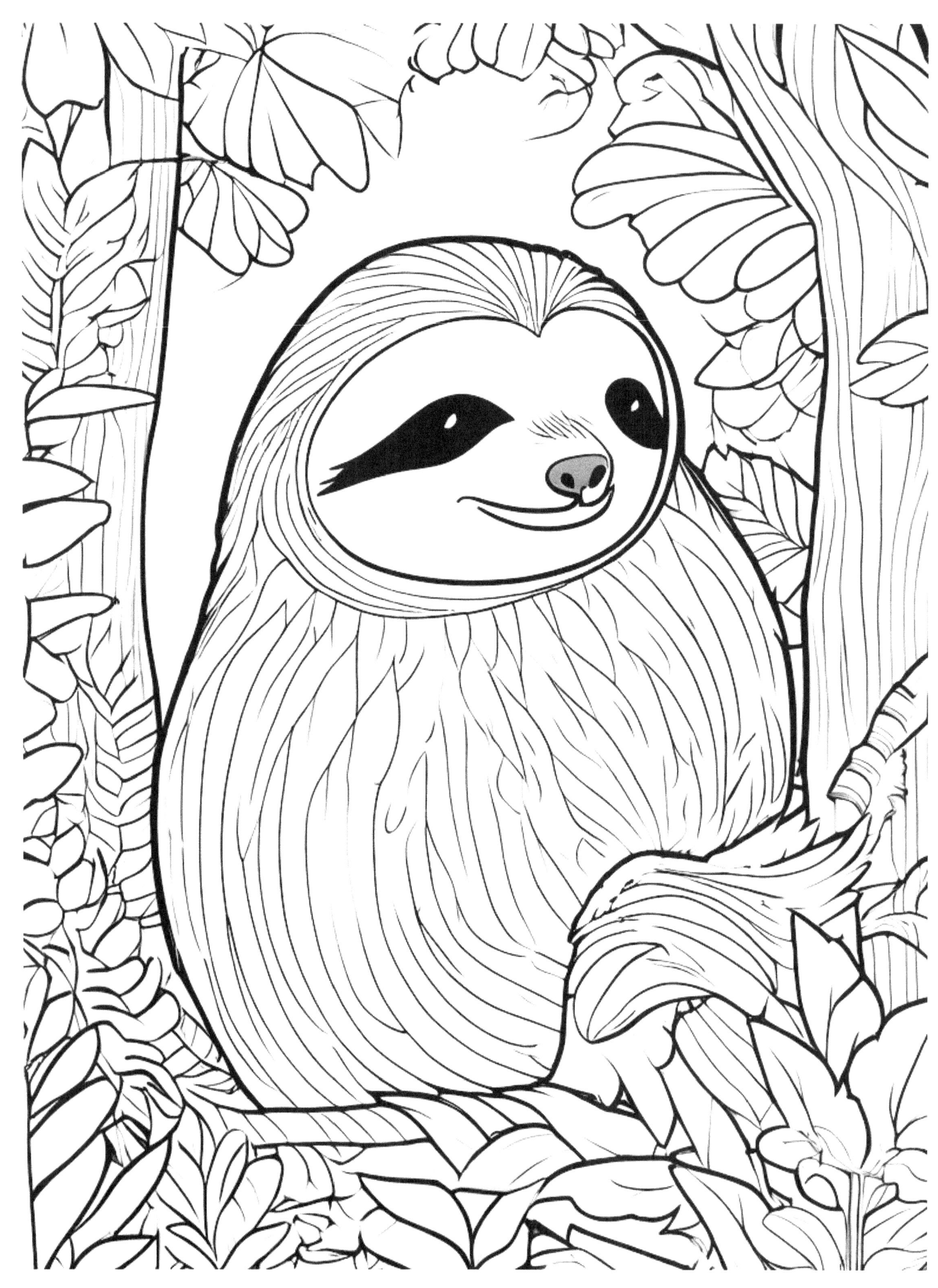

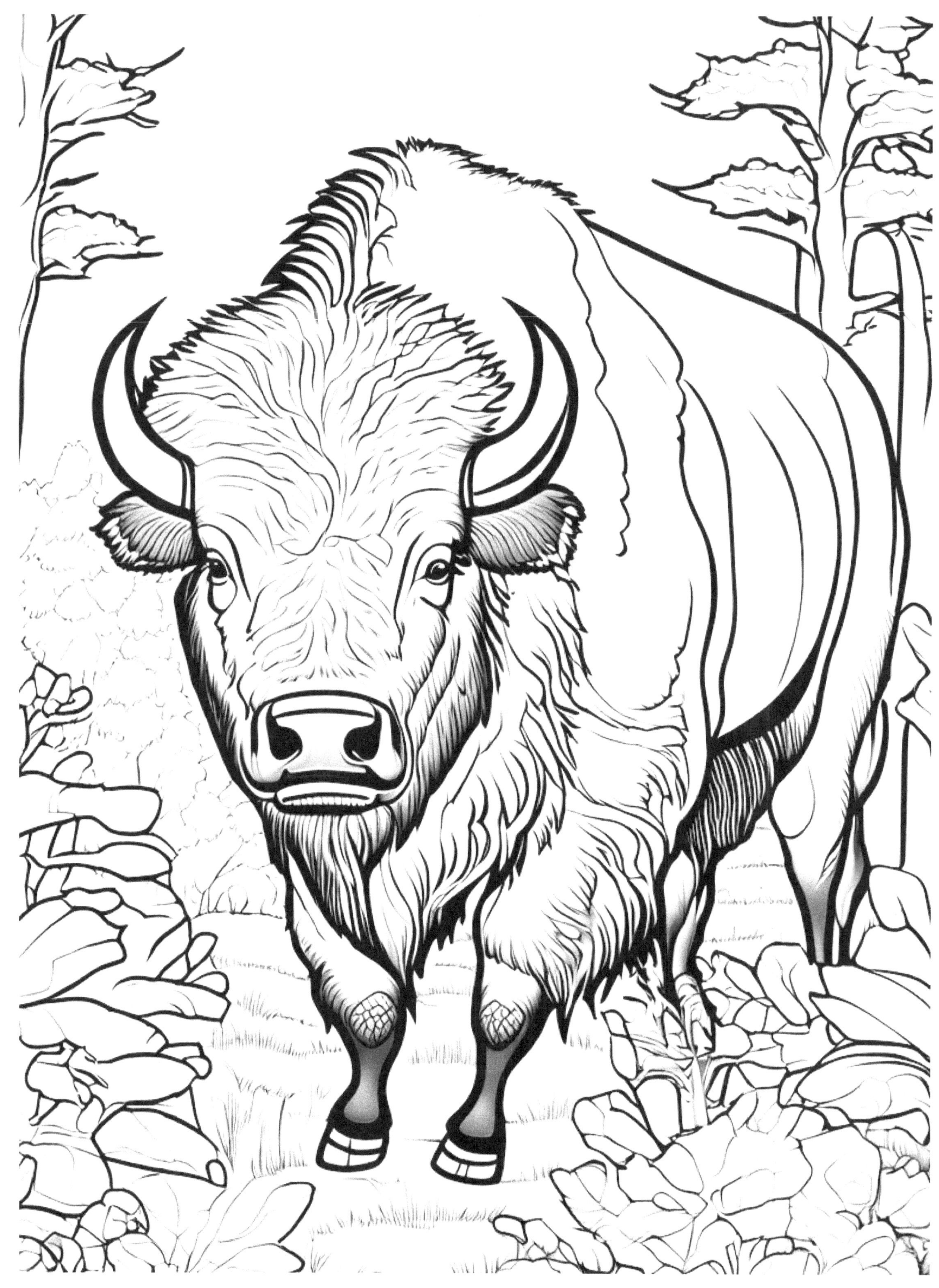

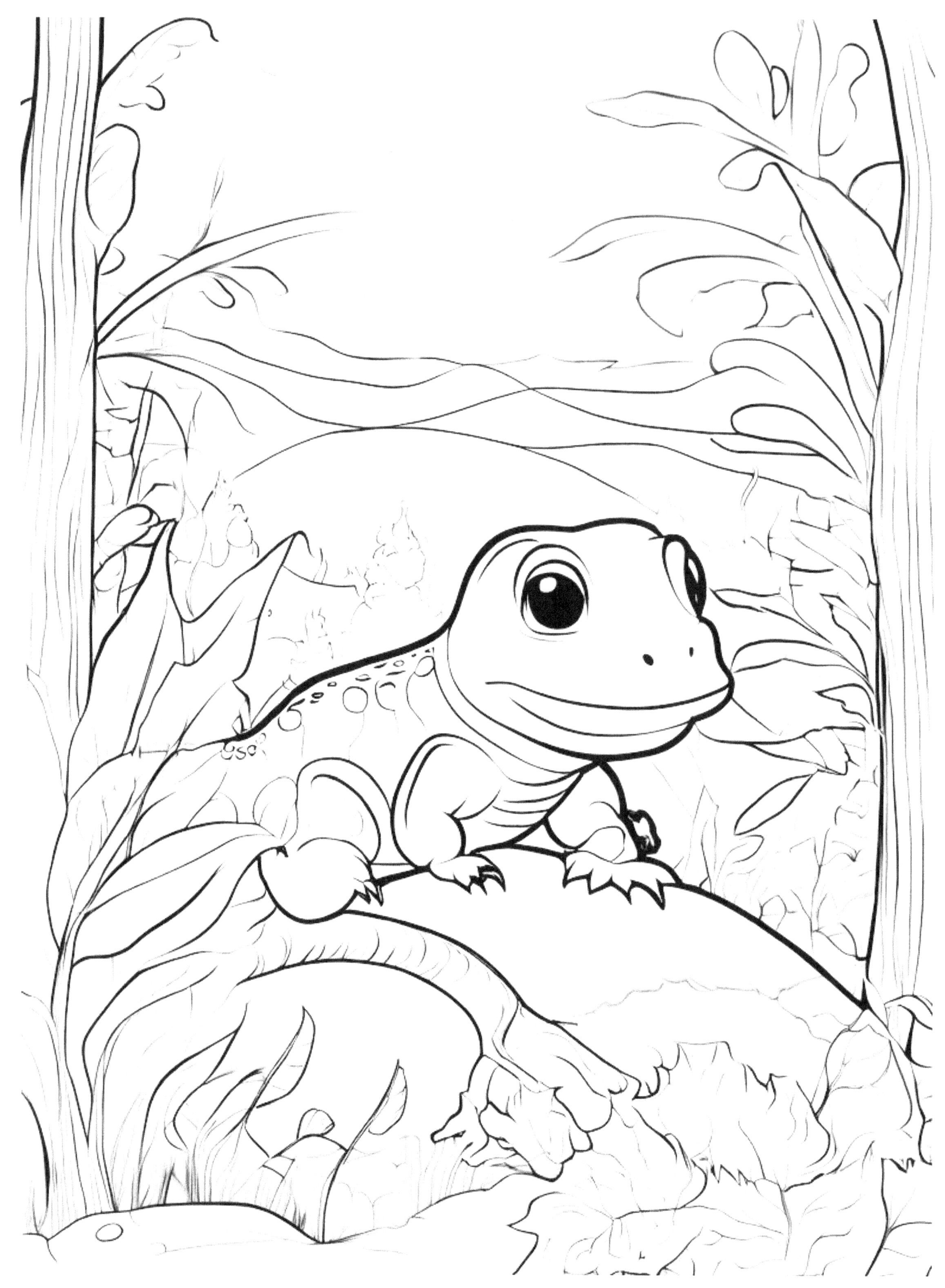

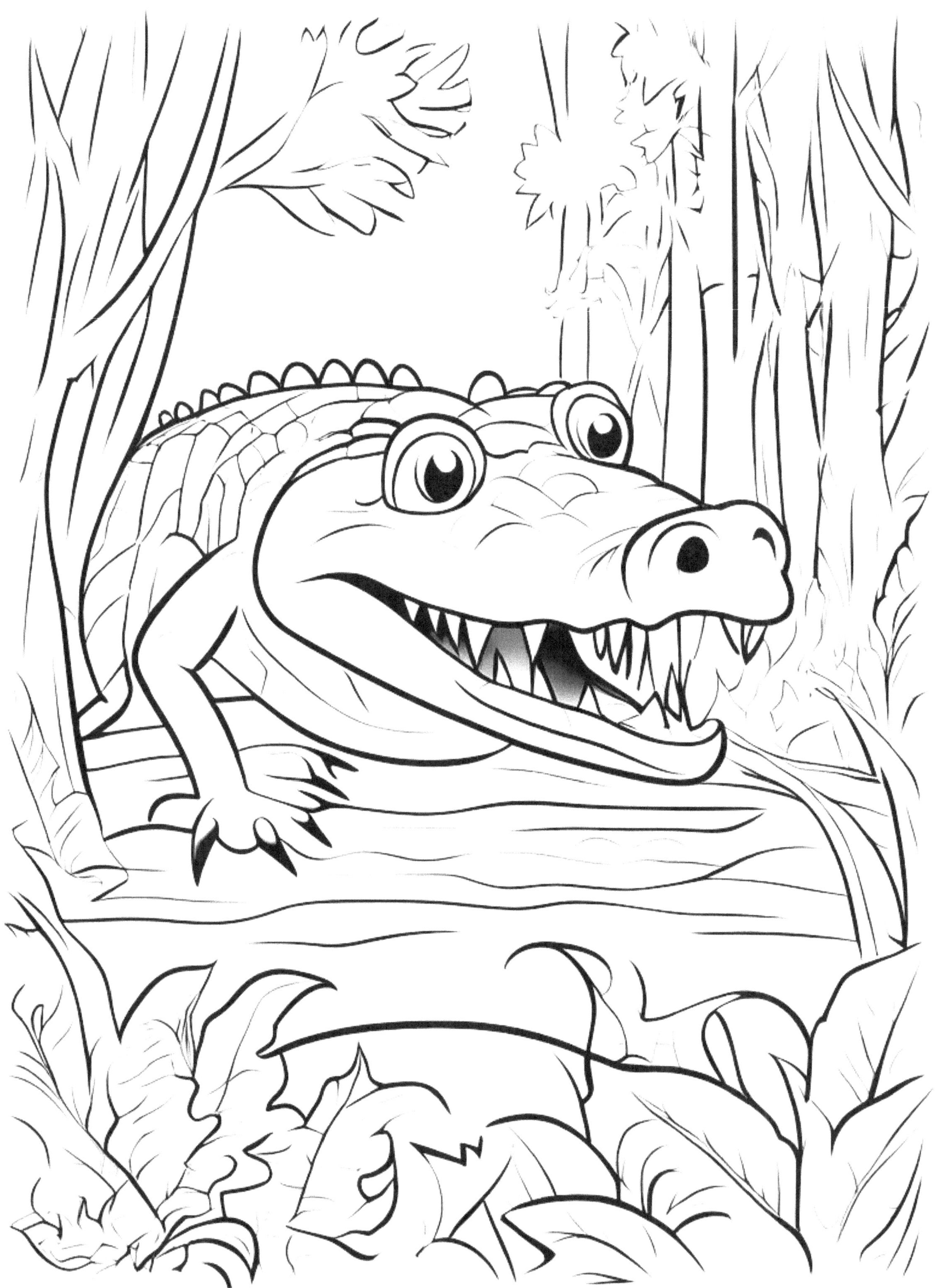

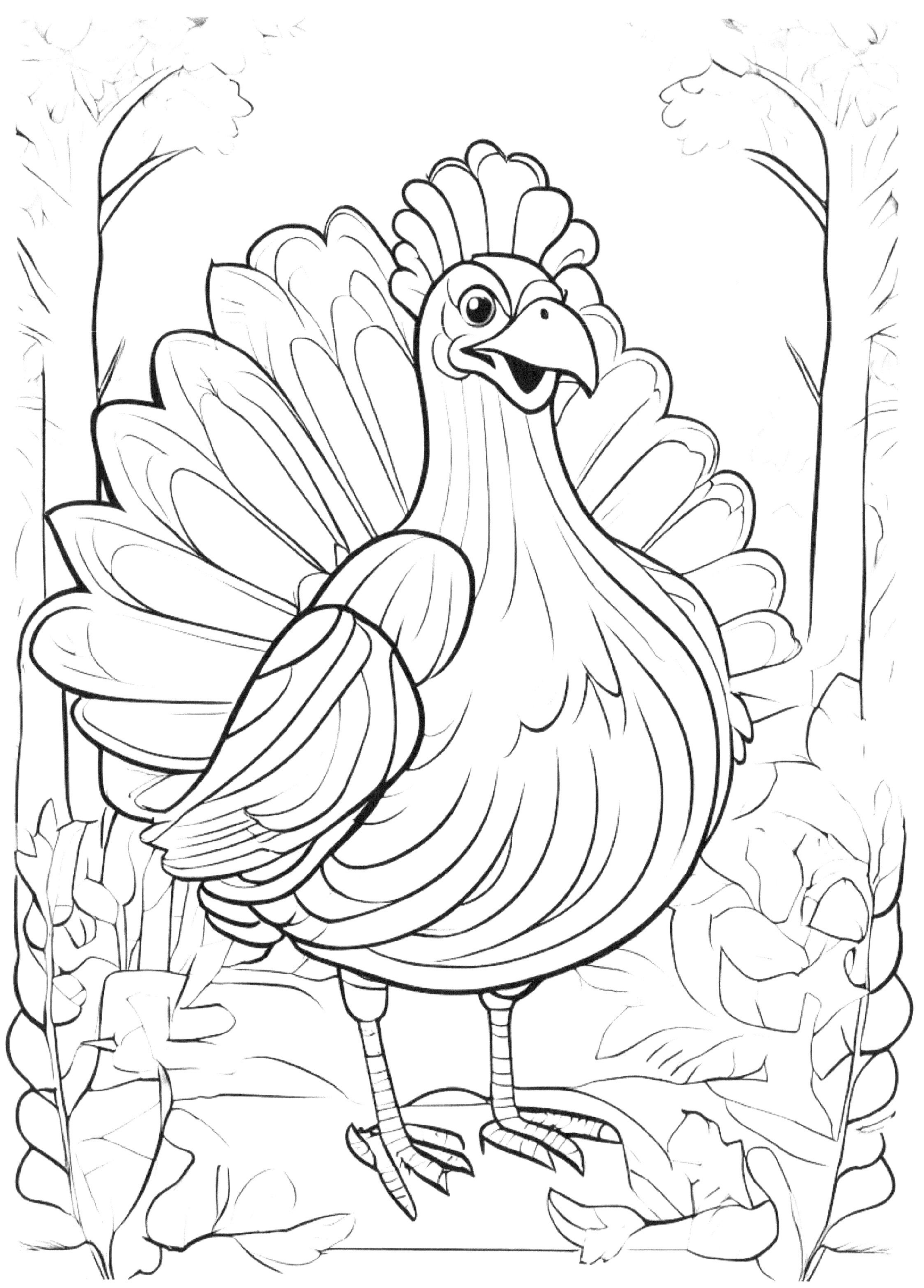